NARCISSISTIC LEADERSHIP

Narcissism has become a contemporary pandemic that seems to have been normalized, accepted, and even celebrated, both in society at large and by some of our political and business leaders. In this book, world-renowned psychology and leadership thinker Manfred Kets de Vries explains this modern phenomenon and imagines how you would help the narcissist on the notional "coach's couch."

Consumerism, competitive urges, individualism, and identity politics are examples of how our present-day culture has reinforced the self-glorification that drives narcissism—this cult of the self. Although a healthy competitive spirit is part of human nature, for narcissistic people it can turn into an all-consuming character trait. They view the world almost exclusively in terms of "winners" and "losers," and to lose is unacceptable. Unfortunately, social media seems to provide ample opportunities to magnify the competitive or narcissistic disposition present in all of us.

Starting with an in-depth discussion of the ancient myth of Narcissus, the various shapes in which narcissism expresses itself are highlighted. Subsequently, taking individual and group perspectives, various strategies for how to manage narcissistic people are explored. Using case examples of interpersonal and group approaches to change, concepts such as the working alliance, the emotional seesaw, the grey rock approach, boundary management, Socratic questioning, the sandwich tactic, and the need to be empathic are introduced. Also, referring to change in a group setting, the importance of the psychological dynamics of the group-as-a-whole is presented.

Narcissistic Leadership offers a unique and original approach to exploring the ramifications of narcissistic leadership and will be of interest to the general reader as well as the key audiences of organizational leaders, psychoanalysts, coaches, psychotherapists, sociologists, and social psychologists.

Manfred F. R. Kets de Vries is the distinguished clinical professor of leadership development and organizational change at INSEAD and the founder of INSEAD's Global Leadership Center. *The Financial Times, Wirtschaftswoche, Le Capital, El Pais,* and *The Economist* have rated him among the world's leading management thinkers. He is the author of more than 50 books and hundreds of articles and the recipient of numerous awards, including four honorary doctorates.

NARCISSISTIC LEADERSHIP

Narcissus on the Couch

Manfred F. R. Kets de Vries

R Routledge
Taylor & Francis Group

LONDON AND NEW YORK

Designed cover image: Walker Art Gallery, National Museums Liverpool © National Museums Liverpool/Bridgeman Images

First published 2025
by Routledge
4 Park Square, Milton Park, Abingdon, Oxon OX14 4RN

and by Routledge
605 Third Avenue, New York, NY 10158

Routledge is an imprint of the Taylor & Francis Group, an informa business

British Library Cataloguing-in-Publication Data
A catalogue record for this book is available from the British Library

ISBN: 978-1-032-94272-8 (hbk)
ISBN: 978-1-032-93553-9 (pbk)
ISBN: 978-1-003-56985-5 (ebk)

DOI: 10.4324/9781003569855

Typeset in Garamond
by Apex CoVantage, LLC

CONTENTS

ABOUT THE AUTHOR

Manfred F. R. Kets de Vries brings a different view to the much-studied subjects of organizational dynamics, leadership, executive coaching, and psychotherapy. Bringing to bear his knowledge and experience of economics (Econ. Drs., University of Amsterdam), management (ITP, MBA, and DBA, Harvard Business School), and psychoanalysis (Membership Canadian Psychoanalytic Society, Paris Psychoanalytic Society, and the International Psychoanalytic Association), he explores individual and societal existential dilemmas in depth.

A distinguished clinical professor of leadership development and organizational change at INSEAD, he is also the founder of INSEAD's Executive Master Program in Change Management and the founder/director of INSEAD's Global Leadership Center. He has been a pioneer in team coaching as an intervention method to help organizations and people change. As an educator, Professor Kets de Vries has received INSEAD's distinguished MBA teacher award six times. He has held professorships at McGill University, the École des Hautes Études Commerciales, Montreal, and Harvard Business School. He is also a distinguished visiting professor at the European School for Management and Technology (ESMT), Berlin and has lectured at management institutions around the world. *The Financial Times*, *Le Capital*, *Wirtschaftswoche*, and *The Economist* have rated Kets de Vries among the world's leading management thinkers and one of the most influential contributors to human resource management.

Professor Kets de Vries is the author, co-author, or editor of more than 50 books, including *The Neurotic Organization*; *Power and the Corporate Mind*; *Organizational Paradoxes*; *Struggling with the Demon: Perspectives on Individual and Organizational Irrationality*; *Handbook of Character Studies*; *The Irrational Executive*; *Leaders, Fools and Impostors*; *Life and Death in the Executive Fast Lane*; *Prisoners of Leadership*; *The Leadership Mystique*; *The Happiness Equation*; *Are Leaders Born or Are They Made? The Case of Alexander the Great*; *The New Russian Business Elite*; *Leadership by Terror: Finding Shaka Zulu in the Attic*; *The Leader on the Couch*; *Coach and Couch*; *The Family Business on the Couch*; *Sex, Money, Happiness, and Death: The Quest for Authenticity*; *Reflections on Leadership and Character*; *Reflections on Leadership and Career*; *Reflections on Organizations*; *The Coaching Kaleidoscope*; *The Hedgehog Effect: The Secrets of High Performance Teams*; *Mindful Leadership Coaching: Journeys into the Interior*; *You Will Meet a Tall Dark Stranger: Executive Coaching Challenges*;

Telling Fairy Tales in the Boardroom: How to Make Sure Your Organization Lives Happily Ever After; *Riding the Leadership Roller Coaster: A Psychological Observer's Guide*; *Down the Rabbit Hole of Leadership: Leadership Pathology of Everyday Life*; *The CEO Whisperer: Meditations on Leadership, Life and Change*; *Quo Vadis: The Existential Challenges of Leaders*; *Leadership Unhinged: Essays on the Ugly, the Bad, and the Weird*; *Leading Wisely: Becoming a Reflective Leader in Turbulent Times*; *The Daily Perils of Executive Life: How to Survive When Dancing on Quicksand*; *The Path to Authentic Leadership: Dancing with the Ouroboros*; *A Life Well Lived: Dialogues with a Kabouter*; *The Darker Side of Leadership: Pythons Devouring Crocodiles*; and *Storytelling for Leaders: Tale of Sorrow and Love*. Furthermore, he has designed a number of 360-degree feedback instruments, including the widely used *Global Executive Leadership Mirror*, *Global Executive Leadership Inventory*, and the *Organizational Culture Audit*.

In addition, Kets de Vries has published more than 400 academic papers as chapters in books and as articles. He has also written more than 100 case studies, including 7 that received the Best Case of the Year award. He has contributed hundreds of mini-articles (blogs) for the *Harvard Business Review*, *INSEAD Knowledge*, and other digital outlets and is also a regular writer for various other magazines. His work has been featured in such publications as *The New York Times*, *The Wall Street Journal*, *The Los Angeles Times*, *Fortune*, *Business Week*, *The Economist*, *The Financial Times*, *The Straits Times*, *The New Statesman*, *Harvard Business Review*, *Le Figaro*, *El Pais*, and *Het Financieele Dagblad*. His books and articles have been translated into more than 30 languages.

Kets de Vries is a member of 17 editorial boards and is a Fellow of the Academy of Management. He is on the board of various charitable organizations and is also a founding member of the International Society for the Psychoanalytic Study of Organizations (ISPSO), which has honored him as a lifetime member. Professor Kets de Vries is also the first non-U.S. recipient of the International Leadership Association Lifetime Achievement Award for his contributions to leadership research and development. He has received a Lifetime Achievement Award from Germany for his advancement of executive education. The American Psychological Association has honored him with the "Harry and Miriam Levinson Award" for his contributions to Organizational Consultation. For his work to further the interface between management and psychoanalysis, he is the recipient of the "Freud Memorial Award." He has received the "Vision of Excellence Award" from the Harvard Institute of Coaching. Kets de Vries is the first beneficiary of INSEAD's Dominique Héau Award for "Inspiring Educational Excellence." Furthermore, he has been honored with four honorary doctorates. The Dutch government has made him an Officer in the Order of Oranje Nassau.

Kets de Vries works as a consultant on organizational design/transformation and strategic human resource management for companies worldwide. As an educator and consultant, he has worked in more than 40 countries. In his role as a consultant, he is also the founder-chairman of the Kets de Vries Institute (KDVI)—a boutique global strategic leadership development consulting firm with associates worldwide (www.kdvi.com). On a more personal note, Kets de Vries was the first fly fisherman in Outer Mongolia (at the time becoming the world record holder of the Siberian *Hucho taimen* trout). He is a member of New York's Explorers Club and in his spare time he can be found in the rainforests or savannas of Central and Southern Africa, the Siberian taiga, the Ussuri Krai, Kamchatka, the Pamir Mountain Range, the Altai Mountains, Arnhem Land or within the Arctic Circle.

Website: www.kdvi.com

PREFACE

That pride, like hooded hawks, in darkness soars, From blindness bold, and tow'ring to the skies.

—Edward Young

In reality, there is, perhaps no one of our natural passions so hard to subdue as pride. Disguise it, struggle with it, stifle it, mortify it as much as one pleases, it is still alive, and will every now and then peep out and show itself.

—Benjamin Franklin

The idea of writing this book of essays on narcissism originated with seeing Todd Field's intriguing film *Tár*.[1] This movie is the character portrait of a woman who, while defined by the world she believes she has mastered, is also unraveling before our eyes. It's what makes this particular film a genuine tragedy. In fact, this film highlights how narcissistic behavior can be used not only for good but also for bad. Although Lydia Tár does not exactly sell her soul to the devil, she demonstrates that talent is one thing but morality is a very different matter.

The film is the story of a fictional classical conductor at the height of her career who engages in activities that in one respect make her very special but in another contribute to her downfall. It's a ruthless but intimate portrayal of art, lust, obsession, Machiavellian behavior, and power set in the world of contemporary classical music. The film portrays an episode in the life of a self-described sapphic individual who favors a masculine dress style in her everyday life and who wears the pants in her marriage to another woman.

DOI: 10.4324/9781003569855-1

However, it is also the portrait of a specific leadership style that's usually associated with men. In that respect, *Tár* is a universal fable about power, whatever a person's gender may be. It demonstrates how power can corrode people's ideals and fantasies and acts as a timely reminder that those whom we may be tempted to idealize are also human; in fact, all too human. And even though the movie starts off as the chronicle of a brilliant conductor navigating her career, it becomes a study of what happens when the social media and a new public morality merge to thrust someone, given all her warts, into the limelight.

Power can corrode people's ideals and fantasies and . . . the people we may be tempted to idealize are also human; in fact, all too human.

This character portrait shows Lydia Tár's complicated relationships with her family, the other people she associates with, and the industry in which she is working. As the film makes quite clear, she is in the kind of position where hubris pretty much comes with the territory. In this respect, the film illustrates how she not only shapes the music but also manipulates the world she is working in, a modus operandi that eventually turns very sour. The film is essentially the portrait of an artist stuck in a narcissistic megalomaniac bubble, exploiting the people she is dealing with and in the process becoming somewhat self-delusional. On top of this heady mix, we aren't just observing a rollercoaster ride of success and self-destruction but we also become part of a story around #MeToo and cancel culture.

Fictionally, Lydia Tár, the conductor and composer, was a highly successful protégée of Leonard Bernstein—a relationship which had set the stage for her meteoric success. We understand, following a very public interview that's presented in the film, that her career had been a steady ascent through the great orchestras of Cleveland, Boston, and New York to her current position at the Berlin Philharmonic. In the interview, she is described as a virtuoso pianist, an ethnomusicologist, and even a popularizer of music. We also hear that she has a Harvard Ph.D. and belongs to the highly exclusive "EGOT" club, having been awarded an Emmy, a Grammy, an Oscar, and a Tony. What we also learn is that she has recorded all of Mahler's symphonies but one, saving the most momentous symphony for last. This recording, *Mahler's Fifth*, will come out soon, as will her book, *Tár on Tár*—a book that's certain to become a bestseller. What becomes quite clear, watching the first part of the film, is that Lydia Tár is an exceptionally talented woman, who also inspires the people who work with her to scale peaks of greatness.

On the one hand, this celebrated genius is enjoying the best that Western society has to offer: performances at the most renowned concert halls, rendezvous with other famous people, exclusive dinners in star-rated restaurants, and rooms in the most luxurious hotels. Yet, on the other hand, we are shown indications of domestic and professional trouble. Lydia Tár lives with Sharon, the Philharmonic's first violinist, and their young, adopted daughter, Petra. But what's there for all to see is an edginess to her various relationships. Their child is being bullied at school. The orchestra's long-serving second conductor has outstayed his welcome. And Tár's assistant, Francesca, who has her own musical ambitions, looks at her boss with barely concealed irritation. Little by little, it is dawning on us, as the viewer, that what contributes to these negative interpersonal developments is the fact that Tár is, by default, narcissistic. Clearly, Lydia Tár is only interested in Lydia Tár.

Gradually, we come to realize that as well as seeing a brilliant conductor, we are watching a flaming narcissist, swept up in the dizziness of power. Not only is her home life a mess, but we start to become aware of the troubled internal politics in the orchestra—the conflicting personalities and tensions a conductor needs to manage. In her role as some kind of orchestral "CEO," the film shows Tár's imperiousness, her sadistic tendencies, and her Machiavellian talent for manipulating other people. Seeing her in action, it becomes quite evident to the viewer that conducting is *not* a democracy. It much more resembles a dictatorship. And although she has gotten away with her imperial style for a long time, her narcissistic ways of handling her various constituencies have started to become more noticeable to the people who have to deal with her.

With respect to her darker side, Lydia Tár is also a woman of great sexual appetites. Here, one concern in the movie seems to be that sticky problem of how and whether to separate the art from the artist—a problem dramatized when Tár gives a guest lecture at the Juilliard School of Music in New York. During her lecture, she has a dispute with a young, gay, nonwhite conductor in training who is dismissive of Bach on account of the composer's patriarchal lifestyle. This person's criticism gives Tár a great opportunity to make an incisive comment about cancel culture, saying: "Unfortunately, the architect of your soul appears to be social media." The student leaves the lecture hall furiously but not without saying, "You're a real bitch." It's a chastening sequence, illustrative of the conductor's arrogance. But it also demonstrates her killer instinct.

And a "bitch" Tár is. Most likely, as insinuated by this student, Tár would prefer artists not to stand out because of their personal indiscretions, one reason being that she has many indiscretions of her own. It is clear that she strongly believes in the value of art, whatever the moral values of the artist may be. And from this perspective, Tár has many skeletons in her closet. She turns out to be a serial seducer of young would-be female conductors, including a young protégé whom she had pushed to suicide. And in the context of this particular personal trait, the film also shows her scheming to hire a musician who has caught her eye. Eventually, this lustful weakness, and her willingness to use her power and prestige to advance a sexual agenda, becomes Lydia's downfall. But while this tragedy unfolds, the people around her have great difficulties in dealing with a woman too exceptional to submit to the traditional judgments of society. It is a very hard choice to reduce a person with Tár's talents to her sexual discretions.

Given her narcissistic disposition, Tár's wife Sharon describes all of her relationships—except with their adopted daughter—as "transactional." Due to her talent and position, Tár has been able to get away with her destructive narcissistic behavior. Yet, however talented she may be with music and conducting, her success doesn't last. Her modus operandi brings about her downfall. The film reveals how her life has become increasingly chaotic and fragile. But as we all know, the biggest egos are the most fragile.

Despite her steely nonchalance, guilt, shame, and insecurity chip away at her, while simultaneously consuming the people who she interacts with. Slowly, Tár is descending into a hell of her own making. She loses sleep, has seemingly extrasensory encounters, experiences less satisfaction in work, and even is losing friends and lovers. But Tár, given her success as a conductor, keeps on papering over these mishaps. In fact, she has had a long history of getting away with her indiscretions.

The biggest egos are the most fragile.

Looking at her behavior patterns, Tár is a typical narcissist, noting that rules are for others but not for her. What's there for all to see is that she has a great sense of entitlement, including the right to indulge in her sexual indiscretions. In that respect, the world of classical music offers many opportunities. We could even hypothesize that the exalted nature of music—more than perhaps would be the case in other domains—gives the people who work in this area the illusion that to do so is their divine right.

Eventually, however, Tár's past catches up with her. The conductor's transgressions—real, exaggerated, or invented—are discovered, and they turn out to be her downfall. She loses her position, her foundation, and her fame. Moreover, she never gets the opportunity to conduct Mahler's *Symphony No. 5*—the performance that would have been the capstone to her career. To top it all, furious over her sexual indiscretions and Tár's lack of communication, her wife, Sharon, bars her from seeing their daughter.

Following these setbacks, Tár retreats to her old studio and grows increasingly depressed and deranged. Cancel culture (or maybe it's just the treatment she deserves) has reached out and found her, and by the film's end she has hit rock bottom. Eventually, she returns to her modest childhood home on Staten Island, where certificates of achievement bearing her birth name, "Linda Tarr," hang on the wall. We observe her weeping when she is watching an old video recording of the *Young People's Concerts* in which Leonard Bernstein discusses the meaning of music. While there, in her childhood home, her brother Tony arrives and admonishes her for forgetting her roots. And as a "bitter joke," in one of the movie's final scenes, Tár is conducting video game music for a convention full of cosplayers in an unnamed Southeast Asian city. The game? *Monster Hunter.* Paradoxically, the monster has been hunted.

This film poses many questions. How many shoulders does Tár climb on along the way? How many heads does she step on? How many people has she turned to and discarded? Is this what narcissism is all about? Could there have been any other way? It also raises the question whether a narcissistic person such as Tár is to be admired or to be reviled; whether artists should be judged by their work or by how they live their lives.

Narcissism has its own gravity and is sucking us down.

I am using the film *Tár* as a springboard to a series of essays focused on narcissism. The reason I focus on this subject is that we seem to be experiencing a pandemic of narcissistic behavior. Not only can we observe this pandemic in the world around us, but the political and business leaders who direct this world of ours are no strangers to narcissistic characteristics. It is as if narcissism has its own gravity and is sucking us down. While leadership should not be a popularity contest, and leaders should leave their egos at the door, this is certainly not the case. Unfortunately, a leader who become tangled up in their own ego will lose their way.

Of course, narcissism has always been a part of human nature. In today's society, however, the expression of narcissism has shifted with changes in technology. In particular, in relation to narcissistic behavior, social media has and is playing an important role. The rise of platforms such as Instagram, Facebook, Telegram, LinkedIn, and TikTok has created spaces where people can curate and share their lives, emphasizing, often overly so, their achievements, appearance, and experiences. It has contributed to a culture of self-promotion and comparison—a "selfie" culture. The popularity of taking and sharing selfies, frequently with filters and enhancements, can be seen as a manifestation of people's self-centeredness and their need for external validation—activities that promote narcissistic behavior. This constant pursuit of fame and attention also coincides with an obsession with celebrities and their lifestyles. As we are living in a consumer-driven culture, many of these developments take place under the bane of consumerism, where personal possessions and status symbols are highly valued, again encouraging self-centeredness. To some extent, these influential sociocultural developments among leaders and followers explain why, in this book, I have decided to take you on a deep dive into narcissism.

To set the stage for this exploration, I begin this book of essays with an in-depth examination of the myth of Narcissus. Employing a developmental and behavioral point of view, a hard look is taken at this mythological figure, during which related phenomena important in human development, such as the "mirroring" process and the role of "the double," are also explored. The expectation is that by taking a more contemporary look at the various aspects of this myth, we may obtain greater insight into the enigma that is narcissism.

These essays raise several questions that help us unravel the enigma of narcissism. What is Narcissus all about? Why did he behave the way he did? Why was Narcissus so upset when his image didn't return his love? Why did this myth become so important from a cultural perspective, retaining its relevance in contemporary society? Most importantly, what do these psychological dynamics implicit in narcissistic behavior tell us about the way we behave?

In these various essays it is noted that narcissistic behavior can be looked at as a reflexive turning toward the self, as narcissists—given their childhood experiences—have realized that others will not provide for their needs. They seem to struggle with the fact that the rest of the world doesn't revolve around them, that not everything is about them. At the same time, while discussing narcissistic behavior patterns, it is also pointed out in these essays that the human animal, for reasons of survival, has to be somewhat narcissistic. A certain dose of narcissism and self-enhancement is necessary for effective functioning. In fact, a very low level of self-enhancement can be detrimental to people's general well-being.

Narcissism becomes the anesthetic that dulls their feelings of insecurity.

Yet what will be discovered is that narcissistic behavior is far from harmless. The myth of Narcissus is not just about a young man who is full of himself, staring lovingly at his own image in a pool. The story contains much more than that image, and by looking beneath the surface—underneath all the bravura shown by narcissistic people—we will find emotionally crippled souls—individuals engaged in a self-referential discourse, suffering from what can be called an attention deficit disorder. Desperately, they strive to be recognized as important. Narcissism becomes the anesthetic that dulls their feelings of insecurity. Narcissistic individuals will always live with the fear of never feeling extraordinary enough to be noticed, to be lovable, or to belong, and at the corner of their souls hides a tiny, frightened child. In other words, they act in this way to protect themselves against unwelcome truths. Narcissistic behavior can thus be seen as a survival mechanism. Yet, there are consequences. Narcissists, due to their emotional shallowness, are essentially devoid of all empathy or compassion for other people.

> Narcissistic individuals will always live with the fear of never feeling extraordinary enough to be noticed, to be lovable, or to belong, and at the corner of their souls hides a tiny, frightened child.

That said, however, narcissism is complex and inhabits many forms, and in these essays different forms of narcissistic behavior are discussed. A major distinction is made between the constructive and the more reactive types. Connections are shown between narcissistic patterns and leadership behavior. Furthermore, a very destructive form of narcissistic behavior, referred to as *malignant narcissism*, is introduced. People characterized by this more pathological form of narcissism perceive the world as an extremely dangerous place. They care very little about others unless it is all about them. Thus, the objectification of others—viewing other people as mere objects useful to their needs—will play an important role in how they live their lives. They live in a narcissistic bubble. In fact, given their *Weltanschauung*, or philosophy of life, such people will bend or invent a reality in which they remain special despite all messages to the contrary. It is therefore no wonder that, especially in a leadership context, malignant narcissists can have an extremely destructive effect on the people they interact with.

> Although a healthy competitive spirit can be viewed as part of human nature, for narcissistic people it can turn into an all-consuming character trait.

To enable us to better understand how these narcissists function, in these essays the imperative to win is included as a topic of analysis. Although a healthy competitive spirit can be viewed as part of human nature, for narcissistic people it can turn into an all-consuming character trait. As a consequence, they will view the world almost exclusively in terms of "winners" and "losers." To lose will be unacceptable. They *have* to win, whatever the price, and they will be envious of people whom they perceive to be more successful than themselves, ultimately doing anything to surpass them.

In addition, once more diving into Greek mythology, attention is paid to the phenomenon of hubris. It is pointed out that narcissistic people tend to be prone to reckless pride. But even though narcissistic people may be prone to hubris, it is also noted that to be narcissistic shouldn't be simply equated with being hubristic. Although narcissistic people will try to construct a reality that reiterates and reinforces their grandiose personal image, they are not intoxicated by power to the degree that they lose their sense of reality as would be the case when referring to hubris. Hubristic people act in extreme ways, putting no limits on themselves. Thus, while narcissism can be considered to be a more stable quality of character, hubris can be looked at as a transformation of a person's personality that emerges in response to having gathered significant power. While narcissistic behavior will have its dark and bright sides, hubristic behavior tends to represent dysfunctional excess.

> While narcissistic behavior will have its dark and bright sides, hubristic behavior tends to represent dysfunctional excess.

Looking at narcissistic behavior in a leadership context, it is pointed out that being a powerholder makes it more likely that people will act inappropriately— behavior that may have negative, unintended consequences. These narcissists don't "see" what is happening but tend to create their own realities. There is too much dust in their eyes to see clearly. It may be accurate to say that power swells the head and shatters the crown. Taking this observation into consideration, the question will also be addressed as to what countervailing measures can be used to deal with such leaders.

> Power swells the head and shatters the crown.

Turning back to the Greek myths, the relationship between the figures of Narcissus and the goddess Nemesis will also be explored in the context of hubris. While the goddesses Hybris (or Hubris) and Nemesis seemingly stand in opposition to each other, when combined, this pairing can turn into a compatible contradiction. It is suggested that when these two forces are twinned, they seem to mutually reinforce each other, making the combination much stronger than the sum of its parts. Yet, as will be discussed, in a leadership context, all too often people who combine these characteristics can be quite dangerous. In fact, the Hybris–Nemesis (H–N) constellation can transform into an explosive construct, creating a psychological dynamic that can be extremely powerful; one that is especially attractive to people who feel powerless. Thus, what's also explored is how the display of power and agency by H –N leaders can provide followers with a false sense of control over their own existential anxiety, contributing to feelings of despair and loneliness. As a result, followers readily adopt the rhetoric of H–N leaders and willingly surrender personal responsibility. All too easily they seem to be drawn to these leaders, perceiving them as "saviors" who will put right the injustices they believe they have experienced. Unfortunately, however, the relationship between H–N leaders and their followers can be compared with a Faustian pact—a contract with the devil. Often, due to the hypnotic power of such leaders, followers may rationalize and make excuses for dark deeds in the name of a cause.

What will become apparent throughout these essays is that narcissistic behavior can be extremely difficult to deal with. Narcissists are very resistant to change. Nevertheless, taking individual and group perspectives, various strategies for how to manage narcissistic people are explored. Suggestions are made for how to recalibrate their self-centeredness. However, in dealing with narcissists, as far as a "cure" is concerned, it is also pointed out that we should not believe in miracles. After all, true self-actualization, to be a well-rounded human being, requires connection and empathy with others, something that tends to be absent among narcissists. They are too driven toward looking out for number one. For them, the search for admiration is a drug.

> Not only are narcissists reluctant to look at what has made them the way they are, they can be very manipulative, defending and hiding their dysfunctional behavior behind charm and charisma.

Yet, this compulsive desire to be admired is very difficult to handle. And what complicates matters even more is that as this condition is ego-syntonic, narcissists don't recognize the destructiveness of their behavior. Therefore, not only are they reluctant to look at what has made them the way they are, they can be very manipulative, defending and hiding their dysfunctional behavior behind charm and charisma. That said, in these essays, it is postulated that it *will* be possible to take steps to have narcissists reflect on their actions, to make them more aware of their behavior, and to recalibrate their behavior patterns. Using case examples of interpersonal and group approaches to change, concepts such as the working alliance, the emotional seesaw, the grey rock approach, boundary management, Socratic questioning, the sandwich tactic, and the need to be empathic are introduced. Also, referring to change in a group setting, the importance of the psychological dynamics of the group-as-a-whole is pointed out.

Narcissism has become a contemporary pandemic that seems to have been normalized and accepted.

Finally, in these essays, taking more of a macro perspective, attention is paid to the impact of narcissistic behavior on society. Given the fact that we live in a digital age, it is emphasized that social media seems to provide ample opportunities to magnify the narcissistic disposition present in all of us. Consequently, it is suggested that narcissism has become a contemporary pandemic that seems to have been normalized and accepted.

We need to look for intrinsic sources of validation while detoxing from external and superficial forms of validation.

In fact, consumerism, competitive urges, individualism, and identity politics can be looked at as examples of how our present-day culture has been reinforcing the self-glorification that drives collective narcissism—this cult of the self. In particular, social media has enabled us to wear a self-delusional mask when facing the world. However, it is also noted that looking only at mirrors will not be the answer to solve the quandaries that trouble the world we live in. *Internalities*, the preoccupation with what concerns human inner nature (especially ethical or ideological values), trump *externalities*, the activities on the outside that affect other things. It is thus proposed that we need to look for intrinsic sources of validation while detoxing from external and superficial forms of validation. To give meaning to our lives, it is suggested, we need to transcend narcissistic behavior. People can't understand the meaning of life unless they have been able to surrender their ego to the services of their fellow human beings. *Homo sapiens* can only thrive when it has a purpose larger than itself.

> People can't understand the meaning of life unless they have been able to surrender their ego to the services of their fellow human beings. *Homo sapiens* can only thrive when it has a purpose larger than itself.

However, before attention is paid to the macro issues associated with narcissism, we need to start at the beginning with the reason this series of essays on narcissism started opens with the ancient Greek myth of Narcissus, a story that may have been derived from the ancient Greek superstition that it is a bad idea or even fatal to look at our own reflection. And as we may have experienced ourselves, the act of looking at oneself in a mirror can elicit a range of emotions, from self-love and confidence to self-doubt and insecurity. Thus, mirror gazing can be an incredibly powerful tool for changing our perspective and seeing parts of ourselves that are usually hidden as we look out into the world.

> Mirror gazing can be an incredibly powerful tool for changing our perspective and seeing parts of ourselves that are usually hidden as we look out into the world.

NOTE

1   Todd Field (dir.) (2022). *Tár* [film]. Focus Pictures and Universal Pictures.

EPIGRAPH SOURCES

Edward Young (1798/1742–1745). "Night VI." In *Night Thoughts*. London: Printed by C. Whittingham for T. Heptinstall, line 324.
Benjamin Franklin (1940/1784). "Continuation of the Account of my Life, begun at Passy, near Paris, 1784." In *The Autobiography of Benjamin Franklin*. New York: Books Inc.

1

WHAT HAPPENED TO NARCISSUS?

This love-sick virgin, overjoy'd to find
The boy alone, still follow'd him behind;
When glowing warmly at her near approach,
As sulphur blazes at the taper's touch,
She long'd her hidden passion to reveal,
And tell her pains, but had not words to tell.

—Ovid

And still deeper the meaning of that story of Narcissus, who because he could not grasp the tormenting, mild image he saw in the fountain, plunged into it and was drowned. But that same image, we ourselves see in all rivers and oceans. It is the image of the ungraspable phantom of life; and this is the key to it all.

—Herman Melville

I think the world is like a great mirror . . . and reflects our lives just as we ourselves look upon it.

—L. Frank Baum

THE MYTH

When it comes to storytelling, one of the world's most famous tales is the myth of Narcissus. It has inspired countless artists and writers from the dawn of Western civilization: numerous frescoes depicting Narcissus have been found in ancient Pompeii; the theme has inspired painters as diverse as

DOI: 10.4324/9781003569855-2

Caravaggio, Salvador Dali, and Lucien Freud; and novelists and poets, including Stendhal, Fyodor Dostoevsky, Oscar Wilde, Joseph Conrad, and Rainer Maria Rilke, have drawn on the myth in their work. The figure of Narcissus has also featured in cinema, television, and music, and the mirroring process that is an essential part of the myth has intrigued artists such as Leonardo da Vinci, Jan Van Eyck, Diego Velázquez, Edouard Manet, and René Magritte. In addition, due to his behavior, Narcissus has become the namesake of a major personality disorder: narcissism.

There are Greek and Roman versions of the myth, which differ in some detail but are broadly similar. Both agree that Narcissus was the son of the river god Cephissus and the water nymph Liriope, probably conceived through rape. Soon after his birth, Narcissus's mother visited the blind seer Tiresias to ask about her son's future. Tiresias told her that he would have a long life provided "he never recognized himself"—a reversal of the classic Greek ideal, "Know thyself," the words which were carved at the entrance of the Temple of Apollo at Delphi. This suggested impending doom, but there were pragmatic ways to circumvent the prophecy. All Liriope needed to do was to banish mirrors and other reflective surfaces in which Narcissus could see himself.

Narcissus would have a long life provided "he never recognized himself."

The myth also tells us that Narcissus was extremely beautiful. In fact, he was supposed to be the most beautiful person who had ever lived. Both women and men fell in love with him on sight, yet he always responded to his suitors with disdain and contempt.

The Greek version of the myth recounted that one of the youth's most ardent admirers was a man called Ameinias. Narcissus rejected him, as he did all the others, but subsequently, and very coldheartedly, gave Ameinias a sword with which to commit suicide. As he died, Ameinias cursed Narcissus and asked the gods to punish him. His dying wish was heard by Nemesis, the goddess of vengeance and divine justice. According to the myth, Nemesis led Narcissus to a pool in which he saw his reflection for the first time. He was so overcome by his own beauty that he was unable to stop looking at himself and eventually died in misery because he could not have what he most desired. His fixation with his image meant that he was condemned to remain in the underworld forever.

However, the most popular version of the myth was told by the Roman poet Ovid in his book *Metamorphoses*, which introduced to the story the figure of the nymph Echo. A known philanderer, Zeus loved consorting with the nymphs and often visited them. Clearly, the amorous pursuits of Zeus, the king of the gods, made his wife Hera extremely jealous. However, whenever Hera was about to catch Zeus transgressing, Echo was able to distract her attention. Eventually, Hera found out what had been happening and put a curse on Echo: she would never be able to speak for herself again but only repeat the words of others. Ashamed, and struck dumb, Echo disappeared to live in a cave deep in the forest. Here, of course, she came across Narcissus and inevitably fell in love with him. Like he did with all of his lovers, he repulsed her advances. Echo ultimately pined away until only her voice remained, but before she died, she called on the gods to curse Narcissus, who, as a consequence, died from his self-love. Hoping to recover his body, Echo returned to the pool that had led to Narcissus's demise, but in place of his body she could only find a sweet-smelling gold and white flower.

There is, among others, another later, and less popular, version of the myth, told by the Roman geographer Pausanias. In this version, it was not *self*-love that transfixed Narcissus but grief for his identical twin sister with whom he was in love. When she died, Narcissus would go to a spring to look at himself and find some relief for his sorrow by imagining that he saw not his own reflection but his sister's likeness, in turn pining away with grief.

MORAL LESSONS

When all is said and done, like many other myths, the tragedy of Narcissus is really a moral tale that makes clear that pride and self-obsession will always bring about a cruel fate.

The tragedy of Narcissus is really a moral tale that makes clear that pride and self-obsession will always bring about a cruel fate.

The tale warns people not to become enamored of themselves. Clearly, Narcissus never took other people's feelings into account. Other people seemed to be there for his self-aggrandizement, to make him feel important. Consequently, when a reflective trick was played on him and he saw his own image, he didn't realize what he was actually seeing. It seemed to him that he was looking at the only person who didn't fall for his charms. Conceivably, as that person did not react to him in the way he was used to, Narcissus became highly perturbed, making the prophecy of the blind seer Tiresias come true. Due to the lack of response from the image he saw, he ended up in depersonalized oblivion. From that day forth, to remind us of the danger of self-centeredness, the narcissus flower reappears every spring to warn us to keep our ego in check. Self-love comes before a fall.

The story of Narcissus has stood the test of time. Clearly, its message is still relevant in our day and age. It continues to be a moral warning against becoming too self-centered. It tells us that when we allow vanity and arrogance to consume us, we can lose sight of the things that really matter. Paradoxically, by being too wrapped up in himself, Narcissus limited his potential as a human being and ended up an example of arrested development.

When we allow vanity and arrogance to consume us, we can lose sight of the things that really matter.

The myth also reminds us to be aware of the effects our actions can have on others. In that respect, it embodies the "Golden Rule": treat others as you like to be treated yourself. Learn to be empathic and compassionate. Do not act like Narcissus who showed no respect to his suitors or for their feelings.

Several other lessons are embedded in this tragic tale. One is to be cognizant of the emotional immaturity of youth. In all versions of the myth, Narcissus is described as a foolish and selfish *young* man. At this early stage of adulthood, it is common to be obsessed with appearances. A second, implicit message in the myth is that the young need to understand their role in the general scheme of things. They should know that even at their young age their actions will have consequences.

PUTTING NARCISSUS ON THE COUCH

The richness of the myth of Narcissus is apparent on so many levels. Not only does it have enduring appeal as a cautionary tale but when developmental theories are applied to the story it can also elicit rewarding revelations. Imagine having Narcissus on the analyst's couch. Here is a young man of exceptional personal attractiveness presenting us with a history of selfishness and disrespect for others, an inability to form relationships, and no obvious occupation. We discover that he is the child of rape; that he has a seemingly overprotective mother whose feelings toward him are highly ambivalent; that he is self-centered yet apparently lacking in self-awareness. And the lack of understanding of his emotions seems to have led to the creation of narratives that will alter his thinking and result in self-sabotage. Not being emotionally intelligent, he succumbs to unhealthy coping mechanisms. Narcissus seems to have had an oversized ego but an undersized mind. Thus, taking his developmental journey into consideration, what kind of personality disorders might be revealed during his analysis?

Narcissus seems to have had an oversized ego but an undersized mind.

The legacy of rape

Was Narcissus a victim of circumstances? Being the result of rape is a terrible start in life. Rape is an aggressive act of power, dominance, and entitlement over another person, where there is no empathy or compassion for the victim. Narcissus's mother Liriope would have been profoundly affected by the experience and could have had a very ambivalent attitude toward her son.

Clearly, the decision of a mother to raise a child conceived through rape presents serious psychological challenges.[1] The emotional trauma of sexual violence not only affects the mother but can also lead to intergenerational trauma. During pregnancy, the mother might perceive the fetus as an alien invasion of her body, and the association of the child with the rape will affect her capacity to care for it. How the mother metabolizes psychologically the experience of rape could have a major influence on the child's emotional and social development, well-being, and long-term functioning.

Intergenerational trauma could be aggravated by the decision to tell the child about the rape. Children who know they are the progeny of rape might feel responsible for their father's actions and develop strong feelings of shame and guilt. How children will handle this information will greatly affect the development of their coping mechanisms and the quality of their interpersonal relationships. It should therefore come as no surprise that children conceived through rape can suffer from a range of psychological disorders, the most common being posttraumatic stress disorder (PTSD), depression, and anxiety attacks.

The mother's traumatic experience could be reinforced if the child, particularly a male child, physically resembles her rapist. For Liriope, who would have seen reminders of the rape and rapist in Narcissus's face, the prophecy that he would be safe as long as he "never recognized himself" may thus be highly significant. We could even ask whether the prophecy was directed primarily at Narcissus or at his mother. Was Tiresias insinuating that Narcissus's appearance could make her relationship with him very difficult? Would she struggle to separate her positive feelings toward him from the terrible memory of the way he was conceived? Would looking at him cause retraumatization because of his similarity to the rapist?

Given the possible ambivalent feelings of the mother toward her child conceived through rape, the child's developmental path may be quite difficult. A mother might treat the child as a "child of the enemy" rather than a child who deserves to be loved. In addition, children born of rape may have to face social stigma. They may be regarded as carriers of deviant genes and often are ostracized by their families and communities. All of these factors have to be considered in the context of the prophecy of Tiresias. All in all, it is likely that Narcissus's upbringing would have been very far from ordinary.

Apart from the ambivalence his mother might experience about his appearance, Narcissus himself, when he saw his image in the pool, might be reminded of his father's face. Even if his mother had not told him about the way he was conceived, this confrontation with the self could have meant that he would have acquired knowledge of his origins. Perhaps Tiresias anticipated this risk when he told Liriope that Narcissus should not look at himself. Hence, not only should his mother Liriope try to forget the way Narcissus was conceived, but Tiresias might also have thought that it would be better for Narcissus not to know. Again, we can wonder about the implications for negative intergenerational impact.

Helicopter parenting

We are considering a myth, of course, so how Liriope raised Narcissus can only be a matter of conjecture. We have no information about the interpersonal dynamics that might inform our psychological labor. This ancient myth has transported us to a magical world full of gods and goddesses and their complex interrelationships. Whereas male–female relationships between mortals must be considered in their contemporary context, myths reflect the culture as it existed at a particular period in time.

Myths reflect the culture as it existed at a particular
period in time.

However, whether mythical or actual, rape remains a violent act that can have dramatic emotional consequences. It will inevitably affect the mother–child relationship and, from a developmental perspective, can have multiple outcomes.

Let's now consider the practical impact of Tiresias's warning that Narcissus should never recognize himself. Preventing him from seeing his reflection was always going to be a challenge for Liriope, so it's not too much of a stretch to hypothesize that she might have become overprotective. However well intentioned, an overprotective approach to childrearing always invites trouble and can have a serious developmental impact. If Liriope was a "helicopter" parent, Narcissus wouldn't be allowed to make his own decisions and, by extension, wouldn't even be able to make his own mistakes. Even though Liriope might have been trying to save Narcissus from possible harm, she was also depriving him of the ability to become a person in his own right. Her overprotective attitude would have hampered his social development, keeping him from engaging in social situations and restricting his opportunities to learn social skills and build friendships. Furthermore, the safety net his mother provided might may have led Narcissus to develop an inflated sense of self, believing he was more capable than he really was. It could have made him an attention-seeker, needing people to admire him. And even though all the versions of the myth describe Narcissus's arrogance, his arrogant behavior would have been built on a very shaky foundation. Deep down, he may have realized that this sense of self-importance was built on quicksand. In truth, his upbringing meant that he was ill-equipped to deal with adversity in later life. In reality, he was a very fragile, insecure human being.

The young man on the analyst's couch was not only conceived through rape, doomed never to know himself, and developmentally undermined by an overprotective mother—he was also the most beautiful person who had ever lived.

The burden of beauty

The young man on the analyst's couch was not only conceived through rape, doomed never to know himself, and developmentally undermined by an overprotective mother—he was also the most beautiful person who had ever lived. But it would be wrong to see this as a countervailing blessing. Beauty all too easily can become a curse. If people are constantly being told how attractive they are, too much of their self-worth could become tied to their appearance. As a result, they may begin to live in a bubble of blissful self-delusion. People tend to assume that beauty is accompanied by heightened competence and intelligence and may be inclined to project these misleading assumptions onto beautiful people. However, this makes it very difficult for beautiful people to develop a personality in their own right. And from a sexual perspective, they might also wonder what others *really* want from them: "Me or my body?"

Naturally, beautiful people want to be loved holistically but, sadly, their appearance often overshadows every other aspect of themselves. However, no amount of attractiveness can make up for a dysfunctional personality.

Also—something that never happened to Narcissus as he faded away at such a young age—the aging process can be devastating for these people.

> It was a life lived on the surface—all exterior, no interior.

Obviously, a relationship with someone based solely on their looks is doomed to failure, adding yet another ominous angle to Tiresias's prophecy—that appearances can be deceptive. The answer to the question of what lies beneath may well turn out to be "nothing." So, it is ironic that the way his mother raised him created exactly the conditions that made Narcissus so self-involved and simultaneously turned him into a person without substance. The only principle that seemed to govern his behavior was the question, "How do I look?" It was a life lived on the surface—all exterior, no interior. And sadly enough, seeing the image of himself in the water only magnified his self-obsession, turning it into a deadly encounter.

Narcissus loved himself so much that he forgot to truly live, actually dying from selfishness. In that respect, he is the extreme example of the dangers of self-love without self-knowledge and self-awareness. He had no understanding of his own mental states—what he felt, thought, believed, or desired. He never learned to know himself. Familiar only with externalities, his own and others' inner worlds were of no interest to him, leaving little or no room for other people. After all, he needed to understand himself first to understand other people—a quality that he dearly missed.

> Narcissus loved himself so much that he forgot to truly live, actually dying from selfishness . . . he is the extreme example of the dangers of self-love without self-knowledge and self-awareness.

The challenge of separation-individuation

The combination of being extremely good-looking and overprotected, together with the residual effects of their earliest origins, makes it very difficult for people like Narcissus to develop a personality of their own or to achieve true separation-individuation.[2] Consequently, Narcissus's specific behavior can be interpreted as a reflexive turning toward the self. Given his self-centeredness, Narcissus never learned to relate meaningfully to others and his particular developmental trajectory produced a personality with very little emotional and cognitive depth. In other words, what this tale also suggests is that narcissism, in its most basic sense, is a refusal to grow up.

> Narcissism, in its most basic sense, is a refusal to
> grow up.

As a result, Narcissus was emotionally crippled, addicted to admiration, and had no consideration for anyone but himself. If he had been inclined to explore his inner world, he might have obtained a modicum of self-knowledge and insight about many things that couldn't be seen on the surface. He would have been in touch with his feelings, thoughts, fantasies, desires, and values. He could have developed a sense of purpose in life. Above all, he would have acquired a strong sense of self and been able to create connections that would last. Yet these possibilities are also encompassed in Tiresias's prophecy—that any form of reflection—even self-reflection—would be deadly for Narcissus. Falling obsessively in love with his own image without recognizing himself spelled decline and death. Yet, reflection leading to self-knowledge and self-consciousness would mean acquiring insight about himself and his origins, and that could also be unbearable: maybe ignorance was a better option? The closer we look at the story of Narcissus, the more cursed he appears. Any form of self-reflection would have represented a mortal danger to him.

Maturity and well-being

Let's remind ourselves of the myth to which we are applying this analysis. The theme of the story is narcissistic functioning, and it features a person who has had a dark enchantment cast over him, making him live in a seemingly trance-like, narcotic state. His emotional and cognitive development are stifled. Subject–object differentiation—part of human development that concerns the exploration of external people, as well as internal images and the relations found in them—had been halted. Instead, Narcissus seemed to be completely wrapped up in himself. In fact, he never achieved true separation-individuation. He never became a person in his own right. He seemed to have been a case of arrested development.

Separation-individuation is the name given to the process by which internal maps of the self and of others are formed.[3] These experiential maps, or internal representations of self and others, are created through our earliest interactions with caregivers, from birth to the age of three. The process of individuation plays a crucial role in the life of every individual, from infancy into adulthood.

> The ability to individuate—to become a person in one's own right—
> implies the ability to integrate the frustrating and pleasurable aspects of
> experiences with other people.

The ability to individuate—to become a person in one's own right—implies the ability to integrate the frustrating and pleasurable aspects of experiences with other people. If successful, it contributes to the internalization of a stable sense of self. If time-appropriate separation from parents, peers, and other important individuals occurs, a person is able to act independently and transform into an autonomous human being. It is only when we can differentiate that we are able to build healthy relationships with others. If we come through this developmental process satisfactorily, we will acquire self-acceptance, a sense of autonomy, environmental mastery, the ability to create positive relationships, a purpose in life, and the desire to strive for personal growth.

> It is only when we can differentiate that we are able to build healthy relationships with others. If we come through this developmental process satisfactorily, we will acquire self-acceptance, a sense of autonomy, environmental mastery, the ability to create positive relationships, a purpose in life, and the desire to strive for personal growth.

But separation-individuation is always a work in progress. The striving to become more autonomous never stops. Conversely, arrested development can lead to co-dependent behavior; problematic romantic, familial, and professional relationships; and difficulties with independent decision making. People who do not achieve individuation will also be troubled by a sense of aimlessness.

Looked at in terms of separation-individuation, the tragedy of Narcissus was his inability to go through this developmental process adequately. He was unable to develop a secure identity and remained trapped in a loop of self-love. It is no wonder that when he saw his reflection in the pool he could not distinguish between himself and the other.

Even though Narcissus seemed irresistible to everybody and could have had his pick of lovers, he remained blind to the richness and wonder of the real world. Due to his arrested development, he was never able to realize his full potential. Instead, he ended up with only his ego for company. Never having seen his reflection before, Narcissus was unable to recognize his own face in the mirror of the pool. Given his impoverished mental state, he withered and died like the solitary flower that grew in his place, starved by his own isolated existence, plucked from the web of relations that truly could have marked out his place in the world. No one familiar with daffodils and the way they flourish in masses could miss the symbolism of this traditional ending of the myth.

> He withered and died like the solitary flower that grew in his place, starved by his own isolated existence, plucked from the web of relations that truly could have marked out his place in the world. No one familiar with daffodils and the way they flourish in masses could miss the symbolism of this traditional ending of the myth.

Nevertheless, a daffodil remained. As one of the first flowers to bloom at the end of winter, daffodils announce the beginning of spring, signify the end of cold, dark days, and also symbolize rebirth and hope. Does this touch of hope allow us to imagine that, as time passed, Narcissus would have been able to stop looking in the waters of the pool? As the British-American poet and writer W. H. Auden commented: "If it were his beauty that enthralled him, he would be set free in a few years by its fading."[4] So, is there a future for people like Narcissus? Could the mirroring process have led to another outcome? After all, to quote the famous writer and statesman Johann Wolfgang von Goethe, "Behavior is a mirror in which everyone shows his image."[5]

NOTES

1 Glorieuse Uwizeye, Holli A. DeVon, Linda L. McCreary, Crystal L. Patil, Zaneta M. Thayer, and Julienne N. Rutherford (2022). Children born of genocidal rape: What do we know about their experiences and needs? *Special Issue: Global Public Health Nursing*, 39(1), 350–359.
2 Margaret Mahler, Fred Pine, and Annie Bergman (1975). *The Psychological Birth of the Human Infant*. New York: Basic Books.
3 Mahler et al. *The Psychological Birth of the Human Infant*.
4 Wystan Hugh Auden (1948). "Hic et Ille." In *The Dyer's Hand and Other Essays*. London: Faber and Faber, p. 94.
5 Johann Wolfgang von Goethe (1998/1833). *Maxims and Reflections*. Transl. Elisabeth Stopp. London: Penguin, Maxim 39.

EPIGRAPH SOURCES

Various Authors (1826). *Ovid's Metamorphoses*. Transl. Mr. Dryden. London: Printed for the Proprietors of the English Classics, Book III, lines 474–479.
Herman Melville (1851). *Moby-Dick; or, The Whale*. London: Richard Bentley, p. 3.
L. Frank Baum (1911). *Aunt Jane's Nieces and Uncle John*. Chicago: The Reilly & Britton Co. (Published under the pseudonym Edith van Dyne.)

2

MIRROR, MIRROR ON THE WALL

To love oneself is the beginning of a life-long romance.

—Oscar Wilde

Whatever may be their use in civilized societies, mirrors are essential to all violent and heroic action.

—Virginia Woolf

Man is a true Narcissus; he delights to see his own image everywhere; and he spreads himself underneath the universe, like the amalgam behind the glass.

—Johann Wolfgang von Goethe

MIRRORING

The mirror has always been a presence throughout human history. Although historians cannot really ascertain when humans became enchanted by their own reflection, the ancient myth of Narcissus suggests that we must have gazed upon ourselves from prehistoric times onwards. In fact, our Stone Age ancestors were already crafting the first human-made mirrors by polishing obsidian, a volcanic rock. And even before that discovery, their predecessors would also have gazed at their reflections in any shining object—especially pools of water. We can also imagine that their first "aha!" experience of seeing their own reflection must have been mysterious and breathtaking. Prior to the invention of the mirror, we can assume that they would see themselves through other people's eyes. How we are seen by others becomes the mirror

DOI: 10.4324/9781003569855-3

that tells us what we are like and who we are. Our sense of self-worth is in most cases bound up with the worth we have in the eyes of others.

How we are seen by others becomes the mirror that tells us what we are like and who we are.

Of course, people have always been vain. It makes us ask ourselves what it would have been like when the first person invented the mirror. Could it be that people may have spent all day and night just staring at their own reflection? In fact, seeing their own image must have been experienced as miraculous. Naturally, the mirror would become an instrument that not only helps us to better understand ourselves but also gives us a greater understanding of how others perceive us.

The mirror has always been the kind of intermediate space where we can experiment with wishes, fears, dreams, and realities. Staring at our own image in the mirror has always been a means of personal assurance, an assurance of the self—an activity that starts at a very early age. Of course, drawing conclusions about character solely by looking at people's external features, focusing on the exterior, could be a way to avoid looking deeper into one's self. Also, the thing about a mirror is that by staring into it, people are condemned to consider the world only from their own perspective. In fact, we could even go as far as to describe narcissists as collectors of mirrors, each one reflecting back their own image but never truly enabling them to see themselves.

The mirror has always been the kind of intermediate space where we can experiment with wishes, fears, dreams, and realities.

Taking a developmental perspective, from the age of two onwards, human beings can recognize themselves in a mirror, an experience seen as a milestone in the development of a sense of self.[1] However, looking at ourselves in a mirror has always been an ambivalent activity. Our attempts at self-discovery have always been fraught with puzzlement. When we look into the mirror, we might see all the body parts that belong to us but be unable to see ourselves.

We could even go as far as to describe narcissists as collectors of mirrors, each one reflecting back their own image but never truly enabling them to see themselves.

For example, in the myth of Narcissus it can be seen that his first encounter with his self-image happened later in his life, allowing us to speculate about his unique developmental trajectory. Generally speaking, however, people will look into a mirror at a much earlier age. Consequently, having this mirroring experience so late in life, it can be postulated that Narcissus was unable to process what he saw. Instead, he became confused between what was him and what was "the other." What he saw was seductive but also destructive. Thus, as myths tend to contain moral messages, could it be that part of the pain in human life comes from gazing into mirrors?

> When we look into the mirror, we might see all the body parts that belong to us but be unable to see ourselves.

If that were true, it would be no wonder that tales involving mirrors can be very unsettling and even touch on the supernatural. Still, from a storytelling perspective, mirror magic seems to be part of our cultural heritage. Fairytales are excellent examples—we only have to think of the evil queen in *Snow White* expecting her "mirror, mirror on the wall" to declare her "the greatest beauty of them all." In these stories vampires and witches are also said to have no reflection because they have no soul.

> Mirror magic seems to be part of our cultural heritage.

Many superstitions also tend to be associated with mirrors, particularly the belief that a person's soul could be trapped in a mirror. A good example of this kind of superstition is found in Jacques Offenbach's famous opera *Tales of Hoffmann*, where in one of the stories the reflection of the protagonist is stolen. Mirrors were often covered during sleep or illness, given the superstition that a person's soul may otherwise become trapped in a mirror and be unable to return to the body. In some cultures, mirrors were even covered after a death to prevent the soul of the newly departed from being caught in the mirror, delaying their journey to the afterlife.

As the myth of Narcissus has made quite clear to us, the ancient Greeks were wary of mirrors. They believed that looking at their own reflection in the mirror would bring bad luck. However, such ambivalent feelings about mirrors were not just a Greek preoccupation. The Romans believed that breaking a mirror would break the soul of the person who had caused the breakage. What's more, according to their beliefs, it would take seven years for this soul to renew itself, a superstition that lingers on today in the frequently iterated belief that breaking a mirror brings seven years of bad luck. In other cultures, breaking a mirror was believed to signal a death in the family.

> The Romans believed that breaking a mirror would break the soul of the person who had caused the breakage . . . it would take seven years for this soul to renew itself.

Mirrors can also be a medium for visual enhancement and illusory perceptions. When we look into a mirror, we could argue that it is not really our face that we see. We may also see a distorted image that reflects how we think and feel about ourselves rather than an actual reflection. And at a basic physical and experiential level, mirrors can trigger other-worldly experiences and provide far more than simple reflections. Hence, reflected imagery can become a great source for self-alienation at the level of emotion and cognition. Moreover, there are times when looking at our own image can be very disturbing, particularly as we age. We might not like what we see, and as the years pass we may even see our encroaching death.

> When we look into a mirror, we could argue that it is not really our face that we see.

No wonder that looking at our image in the mirror can trigger an uncanny out-of-body experience—a kind of "me, but not me" sensation. This potential for confusion may be another reason for the frequency of malefic themes of fear and anxiety that feature in so many stories about mirrors. Clearly, experiencing our embodied self "objectified" as a projection outside our body onto a flat screen will always be an otherworldly experience. Perhaps that's why, in everyday life, many of us avoid giving more than a quick glance at ourselves in a mirror—we may be reluctant to have anything more than our appearance revealed.

Despite our ambivalence about seeing our own reflections, mirrors also allow us to see ourselves as others see us, making them powerful tools for self-examination. Mirrors force us to deal with ourselves at a much deeper level; they allow us to make sense of our physical appearance as well as our associated thoughts and emotions. And what we see can compel us to compare our external image with the internal image we have of ourselves, making mirrors a highly effective tool for introspection and self-reflection.

Through conscious reflection—finding a balance between our inner and outer worlds—we may be able to find an equilibrium between the spheres of fantasy and reality. In other words, the process of physical self-reflection can encourage philosophical and psychological self-reflection. Consequently, the mirror can provide us with a great impetus for greater self-awareness and self-knowledge. It can be a catalyst in helping us explore our inner theater—a critical journey if we want to live to our full potential and to be able to do all we are capable of.

Experiencing our embodied self "objectified" as a projection outside our body onto a flat screen will always be an otherworldly experience.

For all of us, the first mirror we see ourselves in is our mother's eyes. These early mirroring processes are critical for our emotional and cognitive development. As children, starting with the primary caregiver (usually the mother), all of us learn to understand ourselves through the reflections of the people around us. Again, let us consider Narcissus, the prototypical narcissist we put on the couch earlier. Given the universality of this aspect of human development, we can assume that Narcissus would have been exposed to this form of mirroring even if he was deprived of other means of self-reflection. However, we can speculate that his conception (through rape) and the prophetic pronouncement following his birth were traumatic for his mother, making the kind of mirroring process he experienced somewhat defective.

Through conscious reflection—finding a balance between our inner and outer worlds—we may be able to find an equilibrium between the spheres of fantasy and reality.

Assuming this, we can also presume that the first act of looking at himself in a reflective surface would have elicited a range of intense emotions, from self-love and self-confidence to self-doubt and insecurity. It would have been an extraordinarily transformative moment. Suddenly, Narcissus would have seen parts of himself that had always been hidden. And as his consciousness rose, the tension between consciousness and unconsciousness would have become extremely bewildering. Unable to distinguish the "me" in his reflection from the "real me," Narcissus seems to have become completely disoriented. The moment he first saw himself in a mirror was also the moment he lost himself.

THE DOUBLE

When Narcissus saw himself in the surface of the pool, he was also faced with his double. According to one version of the myth (as mentioned in the previous chapter), he had a real double, in the shape of a twin sister. Interestingly, as a long tradition of narratives that deal with the theme of the double indicate, the archetype of twins often concerns opposites—doubles who together form a whole, with similarities that can be physical, psychological, or both. For example, the works of writers such as Ernst Hoffman, Edgar Allan Poe, Guy de Maupassant, Fyodor Dostoevsky, Robert Louis Stevenson, Oscar Wilde, and Vladimir Nabokov all touch upon this theme. In some of these narratives, the "double" does not really exist and is a projection of the narrator's imagination—an alternative personality or self—created from fear or wish fulfillment. Often, the first person is a highly respectable individual, whereas the second is representative of the individual's wickedness. The alter ego may even perform an antisocial act for which the first character will be blamed. Robert Louis Stevenson's infamous novel, *The Strange Case of Dr. Jekyll and Mr. Hyde*, is a classic example of this kind of story.

The doppelgänger can be viewed as an exploration of two sides of the same personality, presented as opposites and reflecting the complex divisions or contradictions that can exist within one individual. Often, the "darker" part represents characterological themes that most people prefer to deny to preserve a "proper" self-image. In fact, this binary theme can be seen in the way one person abides by the rules and standards set by society, whereas the other follows a basic human desire to satisfy forbidden or irrational impulses, activities that the first prefers not to be aware of.

> The doppelgänger can be viewed as an exploration of two sides of the same personality, presented as opposites and reflecting the complex divisions or contradictions that can exist within one individual.

The psychologist Carl Jung considered the doppelgänger concept in terms of a person's shadow side: that part of us which resides in the unconscious—aspects of ourselves that we prefer not to see but are nevertheless part of us, like sadness, rage, envy, laziness, and cruelty.[2] In other words, our blind spots. However, Jung also believed that these repressed thoughts and feelings are not necessarily "bad." Positive traits can also exist within the shadow; characteristics that have been invalidated or minimized by others, leading us to repress them—they can include creativity, intuition, and sexual preferences. Jung maintained that a complete personality consists of both our positive and negative qualities, pointing out the importance of integration of this "darker" side in becoming a complete person.

In fact, the notion of the double comes from a primitive psychological defense mechanism called "splitting," whereby polarized views of self and others arise due to intolerable, conflicting emotions. It refers to the aspects of personality that people prefer to deny so that they are perceived by others in a better, if less realistic, light. It begs the question, however, of whether we should only show those aspects of our personality that we want others to perceive. And, as suggested before, perhaps it is more realistic to accept that our shadow side is also part of us; by understanding it better, we can obtain greater insight about ourselves. According to Jung, making sense of our shadow self, despite its name, would be a great way to shine a light on those parts of ourselves that need healing and improvement. It's only when these qualities are repressed or denied that they become labeled as negative or shadowy.

In this context, the warning that Narcissus's safety depended on his never knowing himself was highly ominous. What aspects of his shadow self might he have seen when he looked into a mirror for the first time? What opportunities would introspection and reflection have given him to gain more insight into himself? The myth, however, also suggests that Narcissus did not have the psychological resources to recognize himself. Instead, his fate was determined by the more destructive parts of his personality. At the same time, we should be grateful to Narcissus for helping us understand better the behavior of certain individuals. His story not only has enabled us to understand the importance of mirroring and doubling but has also given us a deeper understanding of the nature of narcissism—a legacy that has made this mythological figure immortal. Furthermore, the myth is a warning to all of us not to be caught in excessive narcissistic behavior, a theme that is dealt with in the next chapter.

> Narcissus's story not only has enabled us to understand the importance of mirroring and doubling but has also given us a deeper understanding of the nature of narcissism—a legacy that has made this mythological figure immortal.

NOTES

1   Lorraine E. Bahrick, Lisa Moss, and Christine Fadil (1996). Development of visual self-recognition in infancy. *Ecological Psychology, 8*(3), 189–208.
2   Carl Jung (1912/2003). *Psychology of the Unconscious.* New York: Dover.

EPIGRAPH SOURCES

Oscar Wilde (1894, December). Phrases and philosophies for the use of the young. In *The Chameleon* [Oxford student magazine].

Virginia Woolf (1929). *A Room of One's Own*. London: Hogarth Press.

Johann Wolfgang von Goethe (1872/1809). *Elective Affinities, with an Introduction by Victoria C. Woodhull*. Boston: D.W. Niles.

3

THE NARCISSISTIC TRAINWRECK

She was always planning out her own development, desiring her own perfection, observing her own progress. Her nature had for her own imagination a certain garden-like quality, a suggestion of perfume and murmuring boughs, of shady bowers and lengthening vistas, which made her feel that introspection was, after all, an exercise in the open air, and that a visit to the recesses of one's mind was harmless when one returned from it with a lapful of roses.

—Henry James

Admiration spoils all from infancy. Ah! How well said! Ah! How well done! How well-behaved he is!

—Blaise Pascal

She was not an existence, an experience, a passion, a structure of sensations, to anybody but herself. To all humankind besides, Tess was only a passing thought.

—Thomas Hardy

People often discount narcissistic behavior as relatively harmless. Thinking about the myth of Narcissus, the initial association would be an image of a beautiful young man staring longingly at his reflection in a pool. But as we have learned by putting Narcissus on the couch, there is much more to his story than meets the eye. It is in fact a very complex tale about mirroring, doubling, shadowing, and arrested development. Reflecting on these themes, what needs to be kept in mind is that healthy levels of narcissism

DOI: 10.4324/9781003569855-4

and self-enhancement are necessary for effective functioning in life, and a low level of self-enhancement will be detrimental to our well-being.

Basically, narcissism is now looked at as a clinical behavior pattern that belies a deep sense of emptiness, low self-esteem, emotional detachment, self-loathing, and extreme problems with intimacy. The pain of the narcissist is that, to him or her, everything is a threat. What doesn't surrender in reverence is blasphemous to one's high opinion of oneself—the burden of self-importance. The narcissist reconstructs his or her own law of gravity which states that all things and all creatures must adhere to his or her personal satisfaction, and when they do not, the pain is far more intense than it is for one who is free from the clamors of "I."

> The pain of the narcissist is that, to him or her, everything is a threat. What doesn't surrender in reverence is blasphemous to one's high opinion of oneself—the burden of self-importance.

Often, narcissistic people exhibit a grandiose sense of self-importance, harbor unrealistic fantasies of unbounded glory, feel rage or intense shame when criticized, and have a great sense of entitlement. And although these people may come across as very self-sufficient—as they seem to be quite full of themselves—they may, in reality, be dependent on others to validate what they are all about. They seem to find it difficult to live without an admiring audience. Their great sense of self-importance, however, should be seen as a form of self-protection.

In fact, narcissistic personality disorder (NPD) needs to be looked at as a very troublesome condition, both for the people themselves and for those who have to deal with them. After all, it is a challenge to interact with a person making statements such as, "I don't care what you think unless it is about me." Interpersonally, these people are quite a handful. Clearly, when referring to people with NPDs, we are talking about people who are unable to form deep connections with others. Moreover, *if* there is some kind of connection, it tends to be quite superficial.

People suffering from this disorder seem to be lacking the basic and necessary human quality called empathy. In fact, the essence of narcissism is an inability to see the world from anyone else's perspective. Narcissists seem to live within a closed system, incapable of empathizing or genuinely relating to anyone outside of themselves. They are unable to understand how other people feel. They have great difficulties when it comes to forming and sustaining intimate relationships. The fake self they create is contrived in the absence of any sense of connectivity. Clearly, when people become a means to an end, the feelings of such people aren't appreciated. Effectively, when the healthy pursuit of self-interest and self-realization has turned into self-absorption, other people will lose their intrinsic value and become mere means to the fulfillment of the narcissist's needs and desires. Therefore, it is no wonder that narcissists can be very destructive and dangerous people to be around.

> Narcissists seem to live within a closed system, incapable of empathizing or genuinely relating to anyone outside of themselves.

But, as noted before, although narcissists may come across as being very confident, surprisingly, a key feature of their personality makeup is low self-esteem. In fact, narcissism can also be looked at as an emotional and behavioral defense mechanism that protects these people from the pain of feeling inferior. Hence, it can be argued that narcissism is not really about self-love. In reality, it may be quite the opposite. Thus, even though these people may come across as quite arrogant and self-confident, exaggerating their accomplishments, it is their way of hiding their low sense of self-esteem. The social mask they have put on helps them in the role they are playing. And this social mask thrives on approval. Narcissists need to come across as powerful as they live in fear.

> Effectively, when the healthy pursuit of self-interest and self-realization has turned into self-absorption, other people will lose their intrinsic value and become mere means to the fulfilment of the narcissist's needs and desires.

In fact, their life appears to be built upon falsehoods. Thus, behind all this alpha male or female bravado, they are really like scared children. And as children go, they can behave quite selfishly, defending themselves by thinking that everything in the whole world is all about them. But their rather exhibitionistic behavior appears to have to do with a lingering feeling that they are, deep down, unlovable. This explains why narcissists need the constant love, attention, and admiration of others to survive. Basically, they don't possess enough healthy self-respect to be at peace within themselves, and the feelings they experience are more like self-hatred. This lack of connection between reality and their grandiose fantasies can make narcissists angry, frustrated, sullen, and prone to lashing out.

> Narcissists need to come across as powerful as they
> live in fear.

Therefore, to repeat this particular point, although narcissists may come across as arrogant and extremely self-confident, it is nothing more than a veneer to cover troublesome feelings of low self-esteem. This explains why narcissists always seem to be preoccupied with how glorious they are, whether it is in terms of power, beauty, status, prestige, or superiority—all ways to hide their feelings of low self-esteem. As they cannot produce enough healthy self-respect to be at peace with themselves, they constantly need the love, attention, and admiration of others to survive. They're hiding their sense of insecurity behind this false persona of bravado.

Furthermore, the apparent independence of narcissistic people—behaving like the world is their oyster—is nothing more than an illusion. In reality, they don't feel secure enough to be people in their own right. On the contrary, knowing how much of their behavior is fake, they are highly insecure, a feeling which they can overcome only by presenting a somewhat grandiose self, reflected in getting the attentions of others or by attaching themselves to those who radiate celebrity, power, and charisma. Hence, they are chronically reliant on the opinions of others as a way of creating a sense of self. They are always comparing themselves to other people—their status, their possessions, and how they live—to calibrate their sense of worth and self-esteem. In fact, when narcissists display exhibitionistic behavior, they're looking for admiration in the same way as toddlers do, and for the same reasons. They are desperate for attention. Examples of exhibitionistic behavior include an inappropriate flashy dress code, talking too loudly, or gesturing in expansive and space-intruding ways. In reality, however, the façade they show to the external world tends to be paper thin. If we were to look beyond this façade, it would reveal a very scared person who's guilt and shame ridden, a person not worthy of a relationship with anybody based on real intimacy. But given the scripts that occupy their inner theater, there will always be the threat of being found out, leading to feelings of insecurity that perpetuate the need to maintain a grandiose exterior. Thus, big egos are often big shields for a lot of empty space, and, in that respect, narcissistic behavior can be seen as a type of survival behavior. Hence, although narcissistic behavior *appears* to show the pursuit of self-actualization, narcissists don't seem to realize that *true* self-actualization requires intimate connection and empathy with others.

> Big egos are often big shields for a lot of
> empty space.

For people with an NPD, other people become simply mirrors, useful only insofar as they reflect back the special view they have of themselves and that they so desperately long to see. If that means making others look bad by comparison—say, by ruining their reputation at work—so be it. And as life is viewed as a constant competition, they're also usually riddled with envy over what other people seem to have.

Essentially shallow, narcissists spend an enormous amount of energy supporting and maintaining a completely fake self to compensate for a deep, dark, cold inner void. To maintain and sustain this false persona, they exploit, use, and abuse others, behaviors that rest on the assumption that one cannot reliably depend on anyone's love or loyalty. Instead, narcissists believe that they must rely on themselves for any gratification that life has to offer.

For people with an NPD, other people become simply mirrors, useful only insofar as they reflect back the special view they have of themselves and that they so desperately long to see.

We can also look at the narcissist's need for admiration as a kind of addiction disorder. Clearly, they are strongly addicted to feeling significant. This explains why they need the constant love, attention, and admiration of others. And, like any addict, they will do whatever it takes to get this feeling often. Similar to drugs, attention makes these people feel good by delivering a "hit" of certain neurotransmitters (chemicals that transmit or block the transmission of electrochemical currents in the brain, and they will do whatever it takes to get their next "fix." But, as is the case with drugs, whatever attention they receive provides only a temporary high. Soon, they will need their next "fix." And this constant pursuit will be quite exhausting. Narcissists never feel the attention they receive is enough, so they are always seeking more attention and affirmation from the outside.

Due to the need for this "fix," narcissists tend to be interpersonally exploitative. Because of the singular focus on fulfilling their own needs, especially external needs, they will continuously use other people to satisfy them. When these "others" no longer give them narcissistic gratification, they will be discarded, no matter how much pain this inflicts. Thus, while narcissists can be quite charming, this charm lasts only as long as the people they deal with are useful to them. Narcissists, in fact, see these "others" as impersonal objects; people to be manipulated to fulfill their needs without any regard for the hurtful consequences of their own selfish actions. Yet, eventually, the people who are being "exploited" *will* come to realize what's happening to them. No wonder, then—given this pattern of behavior—that narcissists are always compulsively in search of new people who are prepared to admire them and bolster their flimsy self-esteem, becoming manipulative as a consequence. The narcissist's sense of entitlement means that their own wishes deserve special consideration and will take precedence over those of others. Consequently, when in a position of power, they can become quite dangerous people to be with.

NARCISSISM AND LEADERSHIP

As a caveat, it should be said that the behavioral qualities of narcissists occur with different degrees of intensity. We all, at times, show signs of narcissistic behavior. In fact, as has become clear, all humans need a certain dose of narcissism to function effectively. Depending on the intensity of an individual's narcissistic behavioral patterns, however, a distinction can be made between constructive and reactive narcissism, with excess narcissism generally falling in the latter category and healthy narcissism falling in the former.[1]

> We all, at times, show signs of narcissistic behavior . . . all humans need a certain dose of narcissism to function effectively.

Constructive narcissists are people who have been fortunate enough to have caregivers who knew how to provide their growing children with age-appropriate frustration; that is, enough frustration to challenge them but not so much as to overwhelm them. Such caretakers were able to provide a supportive environment that led to feelings of basic trust and agency. As adults, people who have experienced this kind of parenting tend to be relatively well balanced. They will have a more positive sense of self-esteem, a capacity for introspection, and an empathetic outlook toward others.

Reactive narcissists, however, have not been as fortunate as their more constructive peers while growing up. Instead, they may have been on the receiving end of over-, under-, or chaotic stimulation by their caregivers. They may have been the victims of severe and long-term neglect and a hurtful and abusive upbringing. As a result, in adulthood they are left with a legacy of feelings of deprivation, insecurity, and inadequacy. They are more prone than constructive narcissists to an NPD. Here, what might otherwise be a healthy pursuit of self-interest and self-realization turns into self-absorption. Subsequently, in their eyes, other people lose their intrinsic value and become mere means for the fulfillment of their needs and desires.

Although constructive narcissists can also be larger than life, they are not purely searching for personal power. As much as they are prepared to make the ultimate decisions, they take advice and consult others. As transformational leaders, they inspire others not only to be better at what they do but also to change what they're doing. It is reactive narcissists, however, who have given narcissism its pejorative sense; it is this narcissism that is generally associated with intense preoccupation with the self, exploitation of others, excessive rigidity, narrowness of outlook, resistance to change, and the inability to adapt to the external environment.

Reactive narcissists are the ones who really possess these feelings of entitlement. They are the ones who believe that rules and regulations don't apply to them but only to others. Essentially, they always expect special treatment from these others. Their underlying sense of inadequacy and insecurity means they have developed an exaggerated sense of self-importance and grandiosity and a concomitant need for admiration. They seem to have become the kinds of people fixated on issues of power, status, prestige, and superiority. Unsurprisingly, given the nature of their inner theater, it's far from unusual for reactive narcissists to reach leadership positions. In social settings and any organizational context, they see life as a zero-sum game with either winners or losers. Their need for positions of power can also be driven by their need to "get even" for perceived slights. Vengefulness is a close companion of pride and vanity, and reactive narcissists create their own reality whereby all creatures are expected to comply with what they desire.

Vengefulness is a close companion of pride
and vanity.

Echoists

Unlike constructive narcissists, reactive narcissists aren't prepared to share power. Compromise will be alien to them. As they will not tolerate disagreement or criticism, they rarely consult with colleagues, and when they do, consultation is purely ritualistic. In leadership positions, reactive narcissists tend to surround themselves with "yea-sayers," or echoists. And here we might recall once more the encounter between Narcissus and the nymph Echo, yet another illustration of the richness of the original myth. True narcissists often live in an echo chamber, only wanting to hear what they like to hear. Those who can be labeled as echoists have difficulty asserting themselves and are prone to people-pleasing—often at the expense of their own needs and feelings. Therefore, on a spectrum of grandstanding, echoism would be at one end and narcissism at the other. Reactive narcissists only look out for number one, whereas echoists think very little of themselves. In a leadership context, this can be a very unholy interchange.

Paranoia

Even when things go well, reactive narcissists can be cruel and verbally abusive to the people they deal with. When setbacks occur, they take no personal responsibility. Instead, they scapegoat other people. As they imagine themselves to be faultless, it is inevitable that when they have issues, these *must* be the fault of the others. Since they deny their own badness, it *must* be the others who are bad. They project their own faults onto the world. They never imagine that they could be responsible.

The world of reactive narcissists is split between those who are for them and those who are against them. Theirs is a world with only one version of reality: their own. Some reactive narcissists may tell lies that reach so deep that they end up floundering in their own delusions. Their skewed, paranoid outlook makes them perceive others' comments as personal attacks—even when none were intended—leading to outbursts of rage. Such "tantrums" should be seen as reenactments of childhood behavior, originating from early feelings of helplessness and humiliation. But, given the power that some leaders hold, the impact of their rage on their immediate environment can be devastating. Their tantrums will intimidate their followers, who might themselves regress to childlike, dependent behavior.

> Some reactive narcissists may tell lies that reach so deep that they end up floundering in their own delusions.

Leader–follower dynamics

As we may realize, the two-way process of mirroring—the interaction between the person looking in the mirror and what the mirror reflects—is part of the human condition. This makes for a complex interplay of emotions, memories, and subconscious actions. It also plays out in an interpersonal context, giving rise to transferential reactions; that is, what happens when people unknowingly transfer feelings about someone from their past onto people they interact with in the present.[2] Mirroring and idealizing are prime examples of these transference reactions. And in a leadership context, this process will be par for the course.[3]

The two-way process of mirroring—the interaction between the person looking in the mirror and what the mirror reflects—is part of the human condition.

In the interface between leaders and followers, in stressful situations the followers may experience their leaders as powerful and benevolent parental figures—a reaction due to a sense of helplessness. In this case, the idealizing transference appears to serve as a protective shield. However, the qualities and attitudes that followers attribute to the leader may turn out to be connected to a childhood image of the idealized parent who would protect them from danger and have very little to do with the actual leader. In other words, in the imagination of their followers, leaders may be *transformed* into figures who embody all of the positive qualities these followers wished their important caregivers had displayed—wisdom, strength, kindness, as well as admiration for, and interest, in them. On the leaders' part, this idealizing process will reactivate their grandiose selves, replicating as it does so an early phase of their lives when their caregivers admired their exhibitionistic behavior. Naturally, leaders rarely mind this idealizing process. Indeed, they may find this kind of affirmation by their followers hard to resist. This is seen with many political leaders, who can become addicted to this kind of interchange. It is also representative of the beginning of cult formation.

Far too often, as the narcissistic leader shifts the gears into overdrive while drunk on power, the juggernaut of narcissism creates highly destructive behavior.

Of course, both idealizing and mirroring can also have a positive side. They can generate a bond that creates commitment in difficult times. However, these unconscious psychological dynamics can also be risky, involving temporary suspension of insight and self-criticism resulting in the gradual suspension of reality testing and allowing for unrealistic hopes and fantasies to govern decision making. These interpersonal dynamics can become highly collusive in leaders who are reactive narcissists. They will act to shore up their image rather than serve the greater needs of society.

In situations of leadership, people's egos tend to cloud everything.

And, far too often, as the narcissistic leader shifts the gears into overdrive while drunk on power, the juggernaut of narcissism creates highly destructive behavior. In situations of leadership, people's egos tend to cloud everything, and, sadly, these narcissists are unable to leave their ego at the door. They don't realize that leadership is not about themselves but also about others. The Chinese philosopher and writer Lao Tzu sums this up well:

> The best leader is one that the people are barely aware of.
> The next best is one who is loved and praised by the people.
> Next comes one who is feared.
> Worst is one who is despised.
> If the leader does not have enough faith in the people,
> They will not have faith in him.
> The best leader puts great value in words and says little
> So that when his work is finished
> The people All say, "We did it ourselves!"[4]

NOTES

1 Manfred F. R. Kets de Vries and Danny Miller (1985). Narcissism and leadership: An object relations perspective. *Human Relations*, 38(6), 583–601.
2 Joseph Breuer and Sigmund Freud (1995/1895). Studies in hysteria. *The Standard Edition of the Complete Psychological Works of Sigmund Freud*. Ed. James Strachey, London: Hogarth Press, Vol. 2, xxxii, pp. 1–335; Heinrich Racker (2001). *Transference and Counter-Transference*. New York: International Universities Press.
3 Heinz Kohut (1968). The psychoanalytic treatment of narcissistic personality disorders. In *The Search for the Self* (vol. I, pp. 477–509). New York: International Universities Press; Heinz Kohut (1971). *The Analysis of the Self*. New York: International Universities Press.
4 Lao Tzu (2017/sixth century BC). *Tao Te Ching: The Book of the Way and Its Power*. Transl. John R. Mabry. Hannacroix, NY: Apocryphile Press, Chapter 17.

EPIGRAPH SOURCES

Henry James (1881). *The Portrait of a Lady*. London: Macmillan and Co.
Blaise Pascal (1910/1669). *Thoughts*. Transl. W. F. Trotter. New York: P. F. Collier & Son.
Thomas Hardy (1891). *Tess of the D'Urbervilles: A Pure Woman*. London: James R. Osgood.

4

THE IMPERATIVE TO WIN

There are two tragedies in life. One is to lose your heart's desire. The other is to gain it.
—George Bernard Shaw

All men want, not something to do with, but something to do, or rather something to be.
—Henry David Thoreau

Simplicity is extremely important for happiness. Having few desires, feeling satisfied with what you have, is very vital.

—Dalai Lama

A VESSEL FULL OF GOLD

In this chapter, the focus will be on another important aspect of narcissistic behavior: the need to win. Winning seems to be a behavioral response that shapes narcissists' lives. But although this can be seen as a part of the human condition, to make it all-encompassing, to make it the only thing that counts in a person's life, can turn out to be quite disastrous. Yet, for narcissists, winning provides social recognition and acceptance. From a neurological view, it is as if they are addicted to dopamine, a hormone that is linked to pleasure. Thus, when they win, they will produce more dopamine, which triggers a good feeling in the reward area of the brain, a feeling that they want to experience over and over again. Unfortunately, this addiction becomes perpetual.

Marcus Crassus was a Roman general and statesman who played a key role in transforming the Roman Republic into the Roman Empire. He was

DOI: 10.4324/9781003569855-5

one of the main players in Roman society due to his highly effective political skills. He would do anything to be successful. A good indicator of his achievements was that he held two consulships. But apart from his political skills, he had financial acumen. Thanks to his business wheeling and dealing, he succeeded in becoming the richest man in Rome. In fact, in today's money his wealth would have run into the billions. Eventually, however, his materialistic and political pursuits would bring about his downfall. Trying to match the victories of Pompey or Julius Caesar, Crassus tried to conquer Parthia (now part of Iran), famous for its fabulous wealth (as if he wasn't wealthy enough). Yet, given his ambitions and ego, he embarked on a military campaign that would cost him his life. According to legend, after Crassus's death, the Parthians poured molten gold into his mouth as a symbolic mockery of his thirst for wealth. Marcus Crassus's desire to win at all costs brought about his own downfall.

So, as has been explained before, people with a narcissistic personality and ambitious drive have always been among us. But while a healthy competitive spirit is part of human nature, it can also turn into a character trait that can become all-consuming. Individuals such as Crassus are always competing and striving to be number one. They hate to lose. In fact, they view the world almost exclusively in terms of "winners" and "losers." Not only are they voracious and insatiable but they are also envious of those whom they perceive to be wealthier or more successful than they are. Resentfully, they will do anything to surpass others. Being successful, whatever the cost may be, is what drives them.

> While a healthy competitive spirit is part of human nature, it can also turn into a character trait that can become all-consuming.

As the example of Crassus illustrates, narcissism, greed, and envy may go hand in hand. But the twinning of greed and envy, two of the seven deadly sins, can be devastating. Greed, the constant craving to surpass and accumulate at any cost, is often linked to a sense of entitlement. Greed will also be a bottomless pit. Although greedy people may temporarily be appeased with their latest achievement, many soon return to dissatisfaction, emptiness, and inconsolability. This relentless and vicious cycle of striving to amass and acquire means that they can never achieve a feeling of fulfillment or enjoyment.

> The twinning of greed and envy, two of the seven deadly sins, can be devastating.

Envy is characterized by feelings of discontent or resentment toward others whom a person believes possess what they desire. Envious people always compare themselves with others and begrudge them their success, brilliance, happiness, beauty, good fortune, or wealth, leading to feelings of deprivation and resentfulness. For such people, possessing what is good and valuable will be a vital element to the preservation of ego. Whatever threatens their status in life and calls into question their accomplishments and attainments, defeats or limits them, or prevents them from getting what they want will be experienced as a narcissistic injury. Clearly, not having what others have seems to accentuate their feelings of inadequacy, low self-esteem, and self-pity. And, like greed, envy can contribute to behaviors aimed at undermining or harming those who possess what they desire.

GREED AND ENVY: THE TWIN TERRORS

In more than one way, greed and envy are like identical twins. Both are complex human emotions with serious negative psychological effects. They are also closely associated with the desire to acquire, be it wealth, possessions, status, or recognition. As has become quite clear, people experiencing greed and envy tend to be dissatisfied with their current circumstances. While greed can lead to anxiety about not having enough or losing what one has, envy can lead to resentment and bitterness toward those who possess what one covets. Both drivers are rooted in social comparisons. Greed often arises when individuals compare themselves with others who have more, driving a desire to keep up or exceed them. In the case of envy, a comparison to others who possess what they believe they lack fuels feelings of inadequacy and resentment.

A sense of void, deficiency, or inadequacy often sits at the heart of envy.

Taking an in-depth psychological perspective, greed often originates from emotional trauma, deprivation, and unmet needs. Envious people often use objects or possessions as a substitute for their inner emptiness. Similarly, a sense of void, deficiency, or inadequacy often sits at the heart of envy. Envious people feel inferior, becoming resentful of people who they believe are advantaged. They may go as far as wishing that these people would lose their status or wealth, even taking pleasure from their misfortune and humiliation. Furthermore, at an unconscious level, greed is self-centered, driven by the desire for the personal accumulation of possessions, whereas envy is more other-centered, focused on what others possess.

Clearly, people with these drives are incapable of self-sustaining behavior. The scripts in their inner theater are dominated by feelings of inadequacy or perceived injustice, and they often lack the inner resources to feel good in their skin. As a result, they continuously require renewed gratification to feel satisfied. It is no wonder that narcissistically inclined individuals depend on external sources of support in the form of praise, admiration, and other affirmations to maintain psychological equilibrium. But given their fragile mental state, whatever they obtain is *never* going to be good enough. In that respect, they remain blinded to these drives. Yet, they will not be able to unlock their creative potential, achieve sustainable success, or even be fundamentally happy unless they align their internal and external worlds—unless they are true to themselves. Therefore, to begin the journey of discovering their purpose, people with a narcissistic disposition must focus on what matters to them internally, not externally.

At an unconscious level, greed is self-centered, driven by the desire for personal accumulation of possessions, whereas envy is more other-centered, focused on what others possess.

EVOLUTIONARY CONSIDERATIONS

What needs to be added is that the pursuit of wealth, power, image, and status has always been part of the human condition. In the evolutionary struggle to survive, such endeavors helped to heighten our early ancestors' social and economic status. In fact, as humans, we all experience inner wants and needs that spur the desire to acquire and to possess. In that respect, because wealth has always been an important signifier of status, greed can be considered a biological imperative. The same observation can be made about envy. Therefore, taking an evolutionary point of view, envy motivates people into action to obtain what other people have to build up their social and economic capital. In more moderate forms, greed and envy can lead to positive human experiences, driving people toward their goals and achieving their ambitions. In excess, however, greed and envy can become the basis of ruthless and harmful behavior.

Sadly, as will be explored further in subsequent chapters, narcissism, greed, and envy thrive in our contemporary culture. The very ethos of materialism and capitalism upholds these characteristics in its feelings of entitlement and looking out for number one. But when consumerist and materialist pursuits become all-pervasive, this can become counterproductive to a satisfying and meaningful life.

As humans, we all experience inner wants and needs that spur the desire to acquire and to possess.

EPIGRAPH SOURCES

George Bernard Shaw (1903). *Man and Superman: A Comedy and a Philosophy*. Westminster: Archibald Constable & Co.
Henry David Thoreau (1886/1854). *Walden*. London: Walter Scott.

5

ARE YOU PRONE TO HUBRIS?

He that is proud eats up himself: pride is his own glass, his own trumpet, his own chronicle.

—William Shakespeare

Put aside your pride,
Set down your arrogance,
And remember your grave.

—Ali ibn Abi Talib

He knows nothing; and he thinks he knows everything. That points clearly to a political career.

—George Bernard Shaw

The imperative to win brings us to the topic of hubris, an important factor when dealing with narcissism and leadership. The various elements that come into play that create this kind of narcissistic behavior will take pride of place in this chapter. The example that follows demonstrates how hubris can manifest itself in an outrageous nature in a leadership context.

In 480 BCE, Xerxes the Great, a fifth-century king of the ancient Persian empire, was preparing himself to cross the 1.2-kilometer-long Hellespont Strait—the narrow stretch of water that separated Europe and Asia. He was in a jubilant mood, having just been victorious in suppressing an uprising against his rule in Egypt and Babylon. Now, some 300,000 troops were ready to pour into Greece to avenge the defeat the Greeks had perpetrated

DOI: 10.4324/9781003569855-6

on Xerxes' father, King Darius. To expedite the crossing of his massive army over the Hellespont, his engineers had built a monumental pontoon bridge. Unfortunately, this construction had not exactly turned out as he had planned. Before Xerxes and his troops arrived, a violent storm had descended, completely destroying the temporary bridge. Infuriated, Xerxes took out his anger out on the sea, marching his troops into its midst, where they whipped it three hundred times, poked it with red hot irons, and cursed its existence. Handcuffs were then tossed into the sea to symbolize its required submission to Xerxes' authority. This bizarre spectacle was culminated by his order to decapitate the engineers behind the bridge's construction. After these dramatic actions, the bridge was rebuilt by tying together 600 ships with papyrus and flax ropes to traverse the gap between the two continents. According to contemporary historians, the crossing of the strait took Xerxes' army seven days and nights. Tragically for him, all these efforts appeared to be for naught. In Greece, Xerxes suffered a crushing defeat, ending the Persian's dream of subduing its citizens.

Xerxes' behavior of whipping the sea has been described as an excessive case of hubris, the kind of behavior that's characterized by not only extreme pride and dangerous overconfidence but also, in many cases, a perturbing arrogance. Clearly, Xerxes believed, given his previous victories, that he was capable of anything. To him, a setback was unimaginable. He was intoxicated by hubris.

Hubris seems to be a disturbance that comes from too much success. Hubris (or *hybris*, literally translated as "excess") is a term which the ancient Greeks used to refer to human behavior that was excessive in nature. And as the story of Xerxes amply demonstrates, hubris is both a transgression of human boundaries symptomatic of outrageous behavior and a regression toward delusionary thinking. People suffering from hubris imagine that the way they view the world is the way the world is supposed to be. It also suggests a loss of contact with reality. Hubristic people overestimate what they are capable of accomplishing, often in extreme ways, putting no limits on themselves. Convinced of the "rightness" of whatever they have decided to do, there is no room for criticism, whether it be related to practicality, costs, or the likelihood of success. And even if their efforts end badly, they still believe that they were doing the right thing.

Hubris is both a transgression of human boundaries symptomatic of outrageous behavior and a regression toward delusionary thinking.

Given the outrageous nature of hubristic behavior, the ancient Greeks considered hubris nothing less than a crime. In fact, it was for them an insidious poison. An essential component of the Greek moral code was the notion that all human beings have their limitations. If there were those so adamant as to ignore human fallibility, they should be prepared under such a code to pay a very high price. A good example of this from Greek mythology is the story of Arachne, a talented young weaver who was transformed into a spider when she claimed, albeit accurately, that her talents exceeded those of the goddess Athena.

Therefore, a recurring theme in Greek mythology focuses on people who lose sight of these human limitations and act arrogantly, behaving as if they are one of the immortals. No wonder they had carved above the temple of Apollo in Delphi the ominous exhortations "Know thyself" and "Nothing too much." No common mortal should try to surpass a god in a particular skill or attribute. Doing so would be nothing less than a transgression against the gods, inviting terrible retribution. Consequently, for the ancient Greeks, hubris was inseparable from Nemesis, the goddess of vengeance. Whoever suffered from any form of hubristic intoxication was sure to be punished by her.

Given the outrageous nature of hubristic behavior, the ancient Greeks considered hubris nothing less than a crime.

NARCISSISM VERSUS HUBRIS

Given what we have learned about narcissism, hubristic behavior is often indistinguishable from narcissistic conduct as many of the attributes of hubris and narcissism tend to overlap. In fact, and quite often, hubris and narcissism are used as synonyms of one another. Nevertheless, even though narcissistic people might be prone to hubris, to be narcissistic shouldn't be simply equated with being hubristic. Essentially, there are several differences. As we have learned, narcissists have an inflated view of themselves, preoccupied as they are with fantasies of personal power to garner the approval and admiration of others, which then bolsters and enhances their ego. Narcissists are trying to construct a reality that reiterates and reinforces their grandiose personal image. But, unlike hubristic people, they are not intoxicated by power to that degree that they lose their sense of reality. Thus, whereas narcissism can be considered a stable quality of character, hubris can be looked at as a transformation of a person's personality that emerges in response to attaining significant power. Even though narcissistic leaders like to be the center of attention—by making decisions that are singularly focused on enhancing a positive self-image—as long as their sense of reality remains intact, their narcissism remains "bounded."

Whereas narcissism can be considered a stable quality of character, hubris can be looked at as a transformation of a person's personality that emerges in response to attaining significant power.

This "bounded narcissism," however, disappears when people become hubristic. In the case of hubris, we are dealing with a form of narcissism that's "unbound." As hubristic people become drunk on their power, they engage in excessive behavior, setting the stage for hubris.

In the case of hubris, we are dealing with a form of narcissism that's "unbound."

Hubristic leaders do not need a stage to shine. Their interest does not primarily lie with seeking opportunities to garner attention purely to bolster their self-image. Unlike the bounded narcissist, they will test the boundaries of acceptable behavior in the belief that they are far superior to anyone else. Eventually, their exaggerated self-belief, bordering on a sense of omnipotence—making for reckless and impulsive behavior—will lead to their demise or downfall.

In other words, even though there will be a co-occurrence of hubristic and narcissistic behavioral patterns, narcissism in itself tends to be more nuanced. Although both narcissistic and hubristic people are no strangers to the darker side of leadership, narcissistic leaders can also be quite successful. After all, a leader's high level of narcissism positively relates to *charisma*—the ability to attract, influence, and inspire people. Such a leader's supreme self-confidence, energy, willingness to take risks, skilled oration, and grandiose belief systems can contribute to inspiring and visionary leadership—a behavioral pattern that can make him or her quite successful.

Thus, whereas narcissistic behavior will have its dark and bright sides, hubristic behavior is typically presented in terms of dysfunctional excess. In a leadership context, to be more specific, it places hubris firmly on the dark and destructive side. Hubristic leaders tend to use their power in maladaptive and unproductive ways. The grandiosity of such leaders knows no bounds, ending up in extremely toxic behavior. They will exercise their power to achieve unrestrained ambitious goals, both personal and organizational.

Consequently, from a conceptual point of view, the origins of hubristic behavior and narcissistic behavior are quite distinct. Whereas narcissism seems to be an enduring characteristic that emerges before adulthood, hubris should be looked at as an acquired condition that occurs later in life, triggered by the accession to a position of significant power. In that respect, hubris is a disorder of the leadership position rather than a disorder of the person.

> Hubris is a disorder of the leadership position rather than a disorder of the person.

Generally speaking, hubristic people are highly disrespectful toward others, an outgrowth of their inflated sense of importance and unrealistic assessment of their capabilities. Intoxicated with power, given their prior successes, they begin to overestimate their abilities. Consequently, it makes it more likely that these people will test the boundaries of realistic behavior. As a result, given their lack of constraint regarding how they exercise power, their hubristic activities will come to the fore—Xerxes being a prime example. As is evidenced by their excessive self-confidence, their perception of being infallible, their contempt toward people who criticize them, and their detachment from reality, people subject to hubris suffer from a serious character flaw, an attitude that typically brings about their downfall.

It should be noted, however, that possessing a narcissistic personality will be a contributory factor in developing hubristic behavior. Narcissistic people, when in a position of power, may acquire an elevated sense of self-confidence and an increasing sense of superiority, thereby creating the conditions that reinforce an inflated self-view, an overestimation of their abilities, a sense of entitlement, and arrogant behavior. If these psychological dynamics continue, these people may enter a state of self-intoxication. This makes hubris a pathological expression, a derivative of narcissistic behavior. Hubris might disappear, however, when these people are no longer in possession of significant power. In that respect, hubris should be looked at as an adjustment disorder, not a character disorder like narcissism. It only comes to the fore after a person has attained a position of power.

> Hubris should be looked at as an adjustment disorder, not a character disorder like narcissism. It only comes to the fore after a person has attained a position of power.

Many leaders epitomize narcissism in their personalities but behave hubristically regarding their leadership. Thus, it is no wonder that in the context of hubris some have even suggested the existence of a "hubris syndrome," once more pointing out that it is a personality disorder that's specifically tied to people who have attained leadership positions.[1] And in describing this disorder, it is made very clear that it is fatal not only from a personal perspective but also from a social perspective, where, when left unchecked, it can have disastrous consequences.

HUBRISTIC LEADERSHIP

As suggested, hubristic characteristics are triggered when people acquire a position of power. Typically, they may worsen the longer people hold power and the more power they have accumulated. Being a powerholder thus makes it more likely that people in this position will act inappropriately, leading to negative, unintended consequences. This will be especially the case when a person's decisions and actions have been successful before. Once more, Xerxes' example is illustrative. After having been victorious in Egypt and Babylon, his ego seemed to have become even more inflated to the point of losing any sense of perspective.

Clearly, hubristic leaders, intoxicated as they are with power and prior success, become overconfident in their abilities and overestimate the probability of becoming even more successful. They begin to suffer from irrational exuberance, thinking that everything is possible and underestimating or ignoring what could go wrong. Consequently, when they are in the thrall of hubris, any criticism of the improbability of success will be ignored. In fact, they become unstoppable. Limitations are for others but not for them. Naturally, such an attitude contributes to irresponsible behavior and recklessness and even leads to immoral actions. Hubristic people will transgress, the morality of their actions be damned.

> Hubristic leaders, intoxicated as they are with power and prior success, become overconfident in their abilities and overestimate the probability of becoming even more successful.

One well-known saying, with biblical origins, that captures this intoxication with power is "Pride goes before a fall." Another well-known metaphor referring to the intoxication of power is attributed to the English politician and historian Lord Acton, who noted that "power tends to corrupt; and absolute power corrupts absolutely."[2] And as he made quite clear, this kind of corruption doesn't make for happy endings.

Unfortunately, in our present-day society, we don't have to look far to find leaders suffering from hubris. In fact, one might even say that we're in the midst of a "hubris epidemic." Unable to put the brakes on their own self-absorption, too many leaders appear bent on a path of total self-destruction—with their organizations or countries falling quickly in tow.

There can be key external factors that set the stage for the development of hubris among leaders: the possession of a considerable amount of power, the existence of minimal constraints concerning the exercise of power, and the length of time they stay in power. When such factors are at play, it doesn't take much before a cultural environment of omnipotence surrounds the leader. Political leaders are particularly vulnerable, especially those in dictatorial regimes, because there are few, if any, constraints on their behavior.

In our present-day society, we don't have to look far to find leaders suffering from hubris . . . one might even say that we're in the midst of a "hubris epidemic."

Coming back to Xerxes, when everything is said and done, however, people in positions of power would do well to read this passage written about him by the historian Herodotus:

> For it was not a god invading Greece, but a man; and no man now existed or ever would exist who was not liable to misfortune from the day of his birth—and the greater the man, the greater the misfortune. Their invader, therefore, being only human, was bound to fall from his glory.[3]

Clearly, as said before, power swells the head and shatters the crown. And people like Xerxes, who think of themselves as gods, tend to fall the farthest and the hardest. Sadly, Xerxes hasn't been an exception. Others have gone before him and after him. Many tales have been told and are still told of hubris—some mythological, others legendary, and many concerning real-life events.

Another dramatic example taken from Greek mythology, the tale of Icarus, again illustrates the seductive power of hubris and the inevitable downfall that comes in its wake. Using wings made from wax and feathers created by his father, the master craftsman Daedalus, Icarus became overconfident in his newfound ability to fly. Intoxicated by hubris, he ignored his father's warnings not to fly too low or too high, and the result was inevitable. Flying too close to the sun, the wax in his wings melted and down he came, drowning in the sea.

For contemporary business leaders who have suffered from hubris, the downfall they set in motion does far more than simply melt the wax in their own proverbial wings. The impact of the hubristic-infused scandals initiated by people such as Adam Neumann of WeWork, Sam Bankman-Fried of FTX, and Elizabeth Holmes of Theranos extended to all those who believed in them, destroying their fortunes. Still, the pain incurred by these hubristic business leaders pales in comparison when we consider that wrought by those in politics, the likes of Kim Jong-Un of North Korea, Bashar al-Assad of Syria, or Vladimir Putin of the Russian Federation. The damage that they cause is not counted simply in financial terms but in the numbers of lives lost. This must leave us wondering whether we should ever trust people to have control over others when they are unable to control themselves.

The damage caused by hubristic political leaders must leave us wondering whether we should ever trust people to have control over others when they are unable to control themselves.

In the world we live in we don't have to look far to see the manifestations of such leadership behavior and its terrifying consequences. A recent example of hubris can be seen in the actions of Russia's Vladimir Putin. Due to his hubristic state of mind, his paranoid logic has been unrelenting, believing himself to be the savior of a "holy Russia" against the unholy forces of the Western countries. In his convoluted *Weltanschauung*, Russia seems to be threatened by Nazis and Wokism—a bizarre figment of his imagination. Albeit imaginary, it was such a pathological perspective that encouraged him to start a vicious war, sacrificing the lives of hundreds of thousands of people.

NOTES

1 David Owen and Jonathan Davidson (2009). Hubris syndrome: An acquired personality disorder? A study of U.S. Presidents and UK Prime Ministers over the last 100 years. *Brain*, 132(5), 1396–1406.
2 Lord Acton (1907/1887). Letter to Bishop Mandell Creighton, April 5, 1887. Transcript of, published in *Historical Essays and Studies*, edited by J. N. Figgis and R. V. Laurence. London: Macmillan.
3 Herodotus, Battle of Thermopylae: 7.198–238.

EPIGRAPH SOURCES

William Shakespeare (1901/c.1602). *Troilus and Cressida*. New York: The University Society, Act II, scene 3, line 164.
George Bernard Shaw (1917/1905). *Major Barbara*. New York: Brentano's.

6

THE MACABRE DANCE OF HUBRIS AND NEMESIS

And on the pedestal these words appear:
"My name is Ozymandias, king of kings:
Look on my works, ye Mighty, and despair!"
Nothing beside remains. Round the decay
Of that colossal wreck, boundless and bare
The lone and level sands stretch far away.

—Percy Bysshe Shelley

In spite of Virtue and the Muse, Nemesis will have her dues, And all our struggles and our toils Tighter wind the giant coils.

—Ralph Waldo Emerson

As we have seen, hubris in itself can cause many problems, but to aggravate the matter even further, there is also the macabre dance between hubris and nemesis. To clarify this psychological connection, this chapter will elaborate on this interchange and on another quality that distinguishes excessively narcissistic people. Here, like before, it may again be helpful to start at the beginning.

What Greek mythology tells us is that Hybris, or Hubris, was a minor goddess, the embodiment of reckless pride and arrogance. Not only was she known for her insolent behavior but she was also notorious for lacking any form of self-control. Given her modus operandi, other gods would avoid her

DOI: 10.4324/9781003569855-7

for fear of her outrageous behavior. Nemesis, on the other hand, was the goddess of righteous indignation and vengeance. It was assumed that her retributions provided an equilibrium in human affairs, balancing acts of hubris and injustice with punishment.

As we have seen, the ancient Greeks used stories about goddesses such as these to help them understand human nature and their place in the universe. In fact, the symbolic nature of these two goddesses seems to be deeply rooted in the human psyche, representing constellations of cognitions, memories, images, beliefs, and feelings, influencing the way we behave.

While Hubris and Nemesis seemingly stand in opposition to each other, when combined, this pairing turns into a compatible contradiction. When these two forces are twinned, they seem to mutually reinforce each other, making the combination much stronger than the sum of its parts. In fact, the Hybris–Nemesis constellation can transform into an explosive construct, creating a psychological dynamic that can be extremely powerful and one that is especially attractive to people who feel powerless.

> The Hybris–Nemesis constellation can transform into an explosive construct, creating a psychological dynamic that can be extremely powerful and one that is especially attractive to people who feel powerless.

Taking a look at current world affairs, we can see how political leaders often take advantage of a Hybris–Nemesis constellation, engaging in arrogant and grandiose behavior (Hybris) while also assuming the role of righteous judge (Nemesis). Such leaders can have a hypnotic effect on people, with many becoming entranced by this contradictory and macabre pairing. What adds to their seductiveness is their strong sense of purpose or mission to lead others and "save" them from some impending doom or disaster. Often, the target audience is drawn to the confidence and excessiveness of these leaders and perceives them as "saviors" who will right the injustices they believe they have experienced.

> Political leaders often take advantage of a Hybris–Nemesis constellation, engaging in arrogant and grandiose behavior (Hybris) while also assuming the role of righteous judge (Nemesis).

Leaders who take on this savior role often have a personality type that has a best fit with what has been previously described as the malignant narcissist.

As explained before, these types of narcissists are first and foremost self-centered; they tend to be short-tempered, thin-skinned, and unable to consider the perceptions and experiences of others. What differentiates a malignant narcissist from a more benign one is the pattern of sadistic-like behavior he or she employs to look out for number one. In particular, a lack of empathy and a lack of remorse are key defining features: malignant narcissists will gratuitously harm others while having little or no regret for the damage they inflict.

What has also been mentioned previously is that although there can be many causes for malignant narcissism it is most commonly observed in people who have experienced serious childhood trauma or neglect, contributing to feelings of low self-esteem and a strong need for control. This emotional neglect in childhood contributes to a painful emotional loneliness that can have a long-term negative impact on how some people deal with life. Consequently, hubris becomes a compensatory behavior pattern to counter profound feelings of inferiority and powerlessness and enable self-righteous justification of retributive activities. Informed by their personal experiences, malignant narcissists know how to speak to their followers' own sense of powerlessness and eagerness for a savior who we will set right the wrongs they believe they have experienced. Additionally, given their narcissistic tendencies, they are all too willing to assume the role of an omnipotent and omniscient force to feed their own desires for power and control.

Malignant narcissists will gratuitously harm others while having little or no regret for the damage they inflict.

In fact, Hybris–Nemesis leaders are masters at beguiling people into this macabre dance of Hybris and Nemesis. The displays of power and agency by Hybris–Nemesis leaders provide their followers with a false sense of control over their own existential anxiety and feelings of despair and loneliness. As a result, a state of dependency is created. People adopt the rhetoric of Hybris–Nemesis leaders and willingly surrender personal responsibility and the need to think for themselves. What they don't realize, however, is that leaders of this ilk are just taking advantage of them to fulfill their own existential needs and that blind loyalty to these leaders can have catastrophic consequences.

The displays of power and agency by Hybris–Nemesis leaders provide their followers with a false sense of control over their own existential anxiety and feelings of despair and loneliness.

The relationship between such Hybris–Nemesis leaders and their followers can be compared to a Faustian pact—a contract with the devil. Often, due to the hypnotic power of these leaders, followers may rationalize and make excuses for dark deeds in the name of a cause. Hybris–Nemesis leaders know how to tap into dark, regressive psychological dynamics, bringing out the worst in human nature and, eventually, the interchange between these leaders and their followers may turn into a *folie de masse*, or mass insanity. Entire societies may even spiral down and disintegrate within a reality-proof and hateful value system.

A horrific example is the rise and fall of Adolf Hitler, a leader who would take advantage of this Hybris–Nemesis pattern by tapping into the misery and suffering of the German nation post World War I and propagating and externalizing his own dark look on life. Seduced by his siren's call, the German population followed him blindly into a catastrophic second World War that ended with tens of millions of casualties.

Hybris–Nemesis leaders know how to tap into dark, regressive psychological dynamics, bringing out the worst in human nature.

In this rise to power, Hitler presented himself as a messianic leader. Through the Nazi party, he installed a cultish state through a combination of military discipline and the use of semi-religious symbol manipulation. He led Germany with grandiosity, weaving both material and spiritual aspects into his rhetoric of German supremacy. Warning his followers about internal and external threats, he justified his amassing of power as a necessity, demanding absolute loyalty and claiming that he would control their destiny in the service of a higher purpose. Whatever unspeakable actions he would undertake, Hitler argued that he was doing so for the good of Germany.

Each of Hitler's grandiose speeches was indicative of this messianic quest to "save" the German nation and its people from evils wrought by oppressive outside powers. He would repeat the ideas of German "pride," "dignity," "honor," and "respect"—powerful symbolic words—when selling his dreams of future glory while also evoking indignation at past humiliations and injuries at the hands of others. In particular, Hitler would direct vengeful animosity toward the Jews, to whom he attributed a historic responsibility for holding back the German nation, and thus deserving of retribution.

All in all, Hitler built up a high moralizing narrative to justify the use of extreme force and violence to rectify the wrongs done to the German people and to fulfill a nation's hopes. This included a preference for glorious death over inglorious submission and a willingness to sacrifice himself and others to achieve his vision of German glory.

Although Hitler may have been an extreme embodiment of the Hybris–Nemesis constellation, he isn't alone. To a certain degree, leaders like Donald Trump, Recep Tayyip Erdogan, Victor Orbán, and Narendra Modi, among others, have been following a somewhat similar playbook. However, the most terrifying scenario remains that happening in Vladimir Putin's Russia. What's for all to see is how the country has turned into a despotic state.

Hybris–Nemesis leaders thrive on threat-mongering and confrontation, at least in their rhetoric. They also want constant attention. At the same time, they seek to blame and attack rivals and enemies, arguing that it is they who are responsible for their nations' problems and are obstacles to achieving its hopes and expectations. Unfortunately, while these leaders claim that they have the best interests of the populace at heart, in reality, once absolute power is achieved, the rule of law will fall quickly by the wayside, as well as any well-defined governing order. Eventually, there will only be the whim of the tyrant, preoccupied in pursuing his or her narcissistic aims to conclusion.

Once absolute power is achieved, the rule of law will fall quickly by the wayside, as well as any well-defined governing order. Eventually, there will only be the whim of the tyrant, preoccupied in pursuing his or her narcissistic aims to conclusion.

Given the destructive influence of these Hybris–Nemesis leaders, it becomes of great importance to recognize their ascent. Though they can be incredibly alluring and charismatic, their rhetoric should be seen as a red flag and a warning that following such leaders will eventually lead to perdition. Knowing their modus operandi, therefore, will be helpful to people who have to deal with these Hybris–Nemesis leaders.

How, then, does one identify the emergence of a Hybris–Nemesis leader? First, they tend to be very demanding and confrontational in negotiations, often lashing out when feeling slighted. In addition, such people will be very good at image management.

But what's even more important beyond recognition is *preventing* Hybris–Nemesis leaders from having the support and opportunity to rise to power. Unfortunately, all too often, their rise to power seems to be inevitable. Taking a hard look at humanity, there seem to be too many power-hungry seductive leaders and too many gullible followers. Too often, the population of a country behaves like sheeple. They are too easily influenced, lacking critical thinking.

> What's even more important beyond recognition is *preventing* Hybris–Nemesis leaders from having the support and opportunity to rise to power.

Although it can be quite depressing to see the rise of such leaders in our current landscape, the wise words of Mahatma Gandhi may give us some comfort: "Truth alone will endure, all the rest will be swept away before the tide of time. I must continue to bear testimony to truth even if I am forsaken by all. Mine may today be a voice in the wilderness, but it will be heard when all other voices are silenced, if it is the voice of Truth."[1] In making this statement, Gandhi also made a plea for the power of critical thought. Even though Hybris–Nemesis leaders are adept at polarization and drawing out the darker parts of human nature, Gandhi argued for recalling and rebalancing the dualities—kindness for cruelty, integrity for corruption, honesty for dishonesty, and generosity for selfishness.

As we look into the future, paying attention to the kinds of leaders that are emerging, we seem to be facing a battle between these dualities. Given this divergence, it is up to each of us to make the choices for the future of all humanity. *Doing nothing is not going to be an option.* After all, doing nothing will also be some kind of choice. And as the English novelist and poet George Eliot once said, "The strongest principle of growth lies in human choice."[2]

NOTES

1 Mahatma Gandhi (1951). *Basic Education*, p. 89.
2 George Eliot (1876). *Daniel Deronda*. London: William Blackwood and Co., Book VI, Chapter XLII, p. 253.

EPIGRAPH SOURCES

Percy Bysshe Shelley (1818, 11 January). "Ozymandias." *The Examiner*, London.
Ralph Waldo Emerson (1867). "Nemesis." In *May-Day and Other Pieces*. Boston: Ticknor and Fields.

7

THE MALIGNANT NARCISSIST

Naught pleases but what is shameful, none cares but for his own pleasure, and sweet is that when it springs from another's pain.

—Ovid

"Bravo!" cried Chateau-Renaud; "you are the first man I ever met sufficiently coura-geous to preach a pure system of selfishness. Bravo! M. le Comte, bravo!"

—Alexandre Dumas

Some relationships are like broken glass. It's better to leave them alone than hurt your-self trying to put them back together.

—Anon

THE MINDSET OF A MALIGNANT NARCISSIST

To further elaborate this discussion on narcissistic characteristics, in this chapter the focus is on a special destructive type of narcissism found among reactive narcissists: the malignant narcissist. Unburdened by the pangs of conscience that moderate most people's interactions with others—but with-out going so far as to commit murder or arson—reference is made to peo-ple who may even qualify for the label of "psychopath lite," to distinguish them from the "heavier" ones, like serial killers. As is the case with many very driven people, these malignant narcissists can be found wherever power, status, or money is at stake. Outwardly normal, apparently successful, and often charming, their lack of empathy, shame, guilt, or remorse for what they

DOI: 10.4324/9781003569855-8

do—combined with their vindictiveness—can have serious interpersonal repercussions. And that's particularly the case in the context of leadership.

For their own self-preservation, people should do more to guard against such people, either by identifying them and weeding them out or by avoiding dealing with them in the first place. After all, interacting with a malignant narcissist can be quite costly. While appalling people are difficult to ignore, due to their Machiavellian personalities these individuals can be hard to spot. What makes it even more difficult to identify malignant narcissists is the fact that many of the qualities that indicate mental issues in other contexts may appear appropriate in organizational life. This is particularly the case in organizations that value impression management, corporate gamesmanship, risk-taking, coolness under pressure, domination, competitiveness, and assertiveness. However, what those who appreciate these qualities tend to forget is that these malignant narcissists have no sense of conscience or of loyalty to their colleagues or their organization. Often, they do long-term damage to people and organizations through their deceitful, abusive, and sometimes fraudulent behavior. Yet, because of the way they operate, they are often "hidden in plain sight." Xavier, who is discussed below, is a prime example.

What makes it even more difficult to identify malignant narcissists is the fact that many of the qualities that indicate mental issues in other contexts may appear appropriate in organizational life.

XAVIER: BEHAVING LIKE A SOB

To many people, Xavier showed character traits that reminded them of the protagonists of Robert Louis Stevenson's novel, *The Strange Case of Dr. Jekyll and Mr. Hyde*. He seemed to portray a split persona. One minute he could be quite charming, and the next minute he could fly into an uncontrollable, seething rage. What was clear was that if people wanted to go from being adored to devalued in the blink of an eye, they simply had to do something Xavier didn't like. It is no wonder that his behavior would confuse people enormously. And he was quite clever to conceal who he was and what he was all about. It was difficult to make sense of *why* he was doing what he was doing. It was very hard to figure out what was behind the mask. Clearly, Xavier seemed to get great pleasure in playing mind games.

What people saw on the exterior, however, was a seemingly successful businessman who could be very pleasant to deal with. Unfortunately, this favorable impression wouldn't last for very long. Nobody could be more charming than

Xavier if you reacted to life on his terms. But if that wasn't the case, his attitude could change dramatically. When the charm didn't work, the intimidation would begin. Very quickly, a darker side of Xavier's personality would emerge. He could sting like a wasp with people who had the nerve to disagree with him.

What's more, Xavier always needed to be the center of attention. Whatever topic he broached, it would always be extremely self-referential. It would always end up being about him. Other people would quickly recognize his insatiable need to be admired, to be seen as the greatest in whatever he was doing. If no attention was paid to the things he had to say, he would quickly get bored. And to get attention, he might even resort to outrageous behavior for the seemingly simple purpose of being noticed. What also was extremely irritating was his tendency to be a *Besserwisser*—a person who always knew better. Also, what didn't endear him to people who got to know him was his closed-mindedness. To be open to other people's points of view wasn't part of his *Weltanschauung*. He felt always compelled to inflict his very fixed opinions of the world onto others. People who dealt with him soon realized that once he had made a decision, it was almost impossible for him to change his position. Being wrong was not something that ever crossed his mind. It seemed as if doing so would make him feel totally lessened and humiliated. Thus, whenever possible, Xavier would attempt to "colonize" other people's minds, trying to force them to agree with him—a pattern of behavior that would end up grating on everyone. It is no wonder that the people who knew him better would comment on his rather cynical, and Machiavellian, modus operandi. Whatever he did, what would always shine through was his insatiable ego, his great sense of entitlement.

Given his way of working, Xavier remained a person of contradictions. Many people found it extremely hard to define him. It was never clear what he was all about. Who was the person behind the mask? What was the *real* Xavier like? Was there more to him than just appearances? Were there any principles that guided him except immediate self-interests?

Unfortunately, when pressed on the matter—when Xavier was asked to respond to more personal questions—what became quite clear was that he preferred to stick to more surface conversations. Whatever the situation, Xavier would end up Xavier playing the role of Xavier. He would refuse the invitation to have a more personal conversation, preferring to stick to superficialities. He was like an actor in a play. He always seemed to engage in a stage performance.

Whatever the situation, Xavier would end up Xavier playing the role of Xavier ... . He was like an actor in a play. He always seemed to engage in a stage performance.

Of course, to really get to know what Xavier was all about, these people *should* have been able to enter his inner theater. To understand his character, they would need to identify the scripts that were predominant. But as things stood, they could only try to make sense of the external manifestations of his character. However, if they did have an opportunity to enter his inner theater, they would discover—as is the case with most narcissistically inclined people—a highly insecure individual. They would also encounter a void filled with very dark scripts, a key one of which was to be on his guard, to be ready to lash out. Given the nature of the scripts in his inner theater, the world was a highly dangerous place. It was like he was living in a jungle, a place where he believed that everyone was out to get him. What was of utmost importance to him, therefore, was to prevent this from happening. He should come out on top at all costs, a behavior that made him not a very nice person to be with.

To Xavier, it seemed that life consisted of a series of battles, filled with winners and losers. The inevitable result of these feelings was that he always had to put on a mask. He always needed to appear strong, even though he felt quite insecure inside. But given the way his character was formed, Xavier could *never* show any sign of vulnerability. He perpetually felt compelled to present to the outside world the image of a highly successful individual. Also, given his deep feelings of insecurity, Xavier always needed to be given a constant stream of attention, adulation, and affirmation.

From a young age, it was forever of overriding importance to Xavier to have others acknowledge him, cheer him on, and tell him how great he was. It appeared as if he needed the help of others to fill the emptiness that he felt inside. However, despite his many insecurities, he would never dare to show an inkling of self-doubt. Woe betide anyone should ever see how vulnerable he really was. Consequently, his behavior would always be just the opposite. He would incessantly brag about his various achievements, even though they weren't as glorious as he portrayed them. Xavier seemed to be addicted to feeling significant.

Clearly, given the way Xavier related to others, he was not the kind of person for intimate relationships. His competitiveness, and his need for attention and affirmation, had crowded out any possibility of real friendships. Fragile egos make for fragile friendships. It is no wonder that he never had any close confidants. Xavier seemed to be afraid that if he got too close to people, they might see through him. He was relentlessly haunted by this lingering fear that people would realize that much of his behavior was merely a dramatic performance to impress them. They might even guess that under this veneer of toughness was lurking an incredible amount of vulnerability. And heaven forbid if they could see though him and understand how insecure he really was, that inside of him there was very little substance—he was quite sure that he would be taken advantage of. People would make fun of him. Thus, it was much better to keep them at a distance. It was much better to come across as tough and independent. Hence, given this mantra of needing to be tough, it was impossible for Xavier to show the kind of vulnerability that the true intimacy of real friendships typically requires. To form real attachments—to get close to people—was far too threatening. In that respect, Xavier had a major attachment dysfunction. He didn't have the psychological architecture that enabled him to build deep relationships with other people. In actuality, he never experienced even the desire to do so.

Fragile egos make for fragile friendships.

Consequently, from early in life, Xavier had learned the lesson that any real emotional attachment needed to be avoided at all costs. Given the way he functioned, he thought that it would only complicate what he was striving for. Real attachment would only create indebtedness. It was visible for all to see that the only attachment he ever really cared about was himself. Clearly, real intimacy and care would never be for him. And taking a hard look at his more personal relationships, his wives had always been seen by him as mere sexual objects and his children as mere extensions of himself. If they behaved differently, if they tried to be their own person, he would be outraged. Predictably, having such an outlook on life made Xavier an extremely lonely person.

In light of Xavier's delicate psychological equilibrium, what would always be of utmost importance to him was being seen as a winner. This need had made him a master of self-promotion and hyperbole. He would do anything to get people's attention, happily resorting to exaggeration and exhibiting a rather cavalier attitude with the truth. Another way he engaged in one upmanship, to have people pay notice, was by demeaning anybody who stood in his way. The art of humiliation was part of his repertoire.

Given his need to always have the upper hand—to be a winner—whenever Xavier saw an opportunity, he would pull a fast one on anyone who obstructed him. Whenever the situation allowed it, he would try to take advantage of other people. And, as he believed that it was a dog-eat-dog world where nobody could be trusted, he thought that this was the correct way to go about things. It was another reason why Xavier didn't have real friends. Whatever pseudo friendships he had, they would always be of an opportunistic nature and quite fleeting. Throughout his life, Xavier always saw other people in monetary terms, to be categorized as financial winners and losers. Clearly, what mattered to him above all was looking out for number one; everything else be damned. And to make this quest a reality, nobody should have the nerve to stand in his way.

Xavier's cavalier attitude toward the truth was also a major pattern in all his business dealings. As a businessman, he couldn't be trusted. Whenever an opportunity arose, he would try to take advantage of others. It is no wonder that, as time went by, Xavier had gained the reputation of being completely unreliable and unprincipled, always prepared to break whatever deal had been agreed upon. In fact, whenever it was in his interest Xavier would become a shameless master of "factoids," of creating alternative realities. Whenever a fact didn't suit him, he would change it in such a way that it would fit his particular way of looking at things. Due to Xavier's distorted inner world, behaving in a straightforward manner was never part of his makeup; he was truly a natural when it came to lying. Lying seemed to be his way of life. As Xavier couldn't let go of his need to be admired or recognized, he would tend to invent a reality in which he would remain special despite all messages to the contrary. Nothing was out of bounds. In that respect, principles were for others, not for him. Shocking, melodramatic, confounding lies would always be a regular weapon in his arsenal and, strangely enough, he would end up believing his own lies. In dealing with Xavier, people never knew what was the truth and what was a lie. Of course, while Xavier was trying to fool others, people in the know had figured out that he was just fooling himself.

Given the way Xavier was shaped psychologically, he became the kind of business executive who would say, "When the going gets tough, the buck stops with everybody"—that is, everybody else, but never with him. When faced with failure, Xavier knew how to deflect attention from himself. He knew how to create distractions, to distort what had really happened. When necessary, he would go in all directions to obfuscate whatever went wrong in his business dealings. It would always be the fault of the others: the economy, the banks, competitors, or just bad luck. Taking personal responsibility for a mishap would never come to mind. In fact, Xavier had fine-tuned the art of always blaming others when things didn't turn out as expected. At the same time, you could count on him to be the first to take credit when things turned out right. Clearly, for Xavier the narcissist, nothing strengthened the ego more than being right. Of course, for him to be right meant that he needed someone else to be wrong.

For Xavier the narcissist, nothing strengthened the ego more than being right.

Notwithstanding all his failings, in his business dealings Xavier would go to great lengths to prop up his image of a bold, brash, self-made dealmaker. In that respect, he was a real fighter. Arguing with other people always seemed to energize him. Fighting made him feel the most alive. His habit of quarreling over even the smallest things appeared to be a fundamental existential need. Xavier would actually *create* fights when he felt that things were too peaceful. Whereas for others the mantra was "I think, therefore I am," for Xavier it had morphed into "I fight, therefore I am." He had learned the value of turning the passive into the active. Instead of waiting for things to happen, he would *make* them happen. Throughout his life, *protective retaliation*—lashing out at people he viewed as potential adversaries—became a rallying cry. In his business dealings, Xavier would file lawsuit after lawsuit, defying those who would hold him to contracts. And, as he would say publicly many times, when someone attacks him, he will *always* attack back, but he'll do it a hundred times more.

What people soon found out was that it is hard to win a fight with someone who only lives in his or her own reality. If challenged about one of his business failures, Xavier would deflect responsibility, casting himself as the real victim. In his preferred arena, the courtroom, he would wield pointed accusations and manipulate the system as a weapon in his ongoing battle *against* the people *he* had wronged. In that respect, he was a master at *gaslighting*, making the truth turn into a fog, rewriting reality. That he could make his victims doubt their perception of reality was a form of mind control.

> It is hard to win a fight with someone who only lives in his or her own reality.

A salient quality that also typified Xavier—the other emotional core around which his personality would constellate—was anger. It was anger that would permeate much of his rhetoric. Anger would always be present, like a live volcano smoldering underneath. And with respect to anger, it was like he had discovered a new contact sport. This simmering anger also seemed to affect other parts of his behavior. For example, whatever little sense of humor he possessed would be expressed in a highly aggressive manner. It would unremittingly be used with the purpose of denigrating other people—it always had a very off-putting quality. If he didn't get what he wanted, his rage could be formidable.

Furthermore, Xavier had a rather paranoid outlook on the world. He saw conspiracies everywhere. And even if there wasn't anything to be suspicious about, he made sure to make it happen. He would spread the seeds of suspicion himself. Naturally, given his endless provocations, there was some truth to the idea that people were out to get at him. Because of his aggressive behavior in business, he was right to envision that people were after him, imagined or real. He had very much taken the expression "only the paranoid survive!" to heart. Given this rather paranoid outlook on life, Xavier was also in the habit of slotting people into rigid categories: those who were for him and those who were against him. On top of this, as a master of divisiveness, he knew how to create drama—both internally and externally. For Xavier, there would never be a middle ground.

Expectedly, given this paranoid outlook on life, Xavier was the first to believe that even his close collaborators might be conspiring against him, a fear that explained why there was a constant turnover among the people who worked for him. Sadly, at times, his suspicion could be excessive. And given his tendency to split the world into "us" versus "them," it wasn't difficult for him to find imagined enemies everywhere. Thus, he would always project onto others what he feared in himself. He would accuse them of many of the things he was actually responsible for. Soon, people in the know discovered that having Xavier take personal responsibility for failed actions would never be part of his agenda.

People who worked for Xavier came to realize that the prescription to get him into a good mood was to tell him continually that he was the greatest. To be able to work with him, they needed to play the role of sycophant. They had learned how to echo what he wanted to hear. To get on his good side, he expected almost worshipful praise from them. In contrast, a lack of affirmation of his greatness could have serious consequences. Thus, not having much of a choice, to keep him in a good mood most people who worked for him went along with this strange process. Privately, however, many of them thought he was still behaving very much like a child. And, like a small child, he would have regular tantrums if he didn't get his "fix." If he didn't get his regular dose of adulation, he would quickly become morose and irritable. This behavior created a bubble around him. The people who worked for him would insulate him from bad news, negative feedback, and pretty much any form of criticism. Yet, the tragic outcome of protecting him from disturbing news was that he was increasingly unable to make the right decisions.

Still, Xavier wasn't completely without better qualities. As a negotiator, he did have certain talents. When needed, he could be extremely tenacious. In trying to make deals, his unusual toughness would shine through. He would always hang in there; he would rarely quit fighting. He knew how to wear the opposition down. At the same time, however, he also knew how to drive them crazy by making one outlandish demand after another. Given his zero-sum game attitude toward life, Xavier always believed that making a deal implied denigrating the competition. Making concessions had never been part of his makeup. Whenever he had the opportunity, he would bargain hard on even the most trivial items of disagreement. And being the talented liar that he was, even if he didn't get what he wanted, he would pretend to others that he had gotten his way. Unfortunately, however, the expression "penny wise and pound foolish" never came to his mind. Frequently, he might have appeared to be the winner, but by taking a very narrow perspective, in reality he ended up being the loser. Most of the people he dealt with never wanted to deal with him again. It never dawned on Xavier, however, that his style of negotiating was not the way to build a good reputation.

All in all, despite his occasional charm when he needed something from someone else, Xavier was an extremely unpleasant person to be with. His inflated sense of self, his need for constant tribute from others, his hypersensitivity to any form of criticism, his shallow emotional attachments, his lack of empathy, his exploitative actions, his coldness and ruthlessness, his rigidity in outlook, his vindictiveness, and his paranoid view of the world were clearly evident. Given his activities, what truthfully could be said about him was that there were failed business ventures, duped clients, ditched friends, estranged family members, and broken marriages. And when things went wrong—which was often the case—he was also known for not honoring his promises, actions that wouldn't bother him at all. Having a guilty conscience never seemed to be part of his psychological makeup, highlighting his psychopathic qualities. But as a master illusionist, Xavier had learned how to pretend. He knew how to externalize his mishaps. Instead of being a successful businessman, he was, in truth, a failure. But despite this reality, he was quite talented in spinning his failures into successes. Clearly, how Xavier mentally rationalized what had gone wrong indicated that he needed to be the winner at all costs. Despite all of his protestations to the contrary, he was really a great con artist, adept at deception and easily able to fool others into believing that he was someone who he was not. In fact, in his attempts to mask his shortcomings, he would tell lies that ran so deep that he would end up drowning in a sea of his own delusions. It is no wonder, given Xavier's operational mode, that most people had a very dark view of him. They were quite uncomfortable in his company. Given his often-unethical, amoral behavior, he was seen as a person without principles.

In his attempts to mask his shortcomings, Xavier would tell lies that ran so deep that he would end up drowning in a sea of his own delusions.

THE QUINTESSENCE OF EVIL

Now that we have gotten to know Xavier, let us delve more deeply into what malignant narcissism is. The social psychologist Erich Fromm first coined the term *malignant narcissism* in 1964, describing it as a "severe mental sickness" representing "the quintessence of evil." He characterized the condition as "the most severe pathology and the root of the most vicious destructiveness and inhumanity."[1] Building on Fromm's ideas, others viewed malignant narcissism as a very severe form of a narcissistic personality disorder whereby grandiosity was built around aggression and the destructive aspects of the individual. According to them, even though all narcissists are self-obsessed, malignant narcissists would be at the top of the scale. Like all narcissists, they have a pathological self-belief—a sense of grandiosity—which demands attention and admiration. They're convinced they're special in some way and want other people to acknowledge it as well. Crucially, however, they also have sadistic characteristics and lack a sense of conscience.

Basically, given the sadistic aspects of their personality, malignant narcissists should be considered as having an extremely toxic form of narcissistic personality disorder. Their personality makeup, apart from ego-syntonic aggressive characteristics (cruel and sadistic elements), also includes antisocial features and paranoid traits. Other characteristics that need to be mentioned are an absence of conscience, lack of empathy, a psychological need for power, and a sense of grandiosity.

As we have seen in the case of Xavier, malignant narcissists are skilled manipulators who use others for their own gain, often without regard for the well-being of the people they manipulate. They have a great need for attention and admiration, and they consider themselves special—a quality they want others to appreciate. They strongly believe that the world evolves around them. But to top all of this, they also have a sadistic disposition, lacking any conscience. They don't necessarily get a great deal of fulfillment from inflicting pain, but they do enjoy the sense of power that it gives them, and they're indifferent to any suffering they might cause.

Malignant narcissists are skilled manipulators who use others for their own gain, often without regard for the well-being of the people they manipulate.

Malignant narcissists display aggression, anger, and hostility toward others, sometimes in response to perceived slights or challenges to their superiority. And with respect to their sadistic characteristics, some malignant narcissists seem to take pleasure in causing emotional or physical harm to others.

Furthermore, as we also saw in the case of Xavier, they are no strangers to paranoia. They can be highly suspicious of others' motives and may see conspiracies or plots against them where none exist. Moreover, again with Xavier being a good example, they engage in antisocial behaviors such as lying, cheating, or even criminal activity. In addition, and what can be named as a key characteristic, they can be very vindictive. Further, whatever they do, there seems to be a lack of remorse. They do not take responsibility for the harm they cause to others. Finally, with the case of Xavier once more being a prime example, due to their extreme narcissism and destructive behavior, they have difficulties in maintaining relationships.

Malignant narcissism is not an officially recognized psychiatric diagnosis in the *Diagnostic and Statistical Manual of Mental Disorders (DSM-5)*, which is the standard diagnostic manual used by mental health professionals, but it is often used in clinical and popular discourse to describe individuals who exhibit extreme and harmful narcissistic traits.[2] Although the psychoanalyst Otto Kernberg suggested that malignant narcissism be made a specific psychiatric diagnosis, to date it has not been classified in this way.[3] However, given the manner in which malignant narcissists behave, the terms *malignant narcissism* and *psychopathy* are often used interchangeably. Hence, malignant narcissism should be considered part of a narcissistic spectrum whereby malignant narcissism would be at the high end and narcissistic personality disorder at the low end. While people with a narcissistic personality disorder might deliberately damage other people in pursuit of their own selfish desires, they may regret whatever they have done. In fact, they may even show remorse for having done so. In contrast, the malignant narcissist has a more pervasive lack of empathy than someone with a narcissistic personality disorder alone. As seen in the case of Xavier, they lack the feelings of guilt or remorse for the damage they may have caused. They may even derive pleasure from the gratuitous infliction of mental or physical pain on others. In addition, their neediness can become a grind. They have a constant need for self-aggrandizement as a defense against feelings of emptiness and imagined narcissistic injuries. But even while they're trying to fool others, they're really just fooling themselves. In that respect, they have a major attachment dysfunction due to the way they were treated during their childhood. Malignant narcissists pursue a form of self-actualization but without the realization that true self-actualization requires connection and empathy with others.

Malignant narcissists pursue a form of self-actualization but without the realization that true self-actualization requires connection and empathy with others.

The kind of behavior that malignant narcissists display is a reflexive turning toward the self as a result of childhood experiences which taught them that others would not provide for their needs. Consequently, they don't trust that others will be there for them, so they have to be there for themselves. This doesn't leave much room for anyone else. And as has been said about narcissists in general, because they have poorly regulated sense of self, deep inside they feel quite vulnerable. They are consumed with conveying a shallow false self to others. They're emotionally crippled souls who are addicted to attention. They don't have the ability to feel secure and worthy without external validation and praise. Most of the time, narcissistic traits allow one to hide, defend, or deny these deep insecurities. Whatever positive things are said about the narcissist, they never seem to be good enough. Instead, these messages must be repeated over and over again. Taking excessive credit for any success, while blaming others for their failures, only seems to temporarily lift their spirits.

Malignant narcissists can be labeled as damaged people, often stuck in a delusional spin around their own greatness. Those acquainted with such people would comment that their egos had become insatiable, not realizing that for malignant narcissists, narcissism and self-deception are survival mechanisms. They are chronically reliant on the opinions of others to form their own sense of self and are always comparing themselves, their status, their possessions, and their lives to other people to determine their sense of self-worth.

Since, deep down, narcissists generally feel themselves to be faultless—a way of dealing with past hurts—it is inevitable that when they are in conflict with the world, they invariably perceive the conflict as the world's fault. Dealing with them is like walking on eggshells. There is always the threat that they may get found out, which explains their need to maintain a grandiose exterior. At any moment there could be a breach. Thus, dealing with someone who exhibits narcissism, particularly of the malignant form, can be quite challenging.

It is highly unlikely for people like Xavier to work on themselves; that is, to seek self-help. They will be extremely reluctant to deal with the scripts in their inner theater that fundamentally make them such difficult people to live with. They don't want to look beneath the surface. "Know thyself" is not the credo of a malignant narcissist. To look into themselves, to find out what they are all about, is never for them—it is just too scary. They will argue that any form of psychological introspection is for weaklings. Given their personality makeup, it is mission impossible for malignant narcissists to behave in a reasonable, empathic, or human way. And, if they seem to behave in this manner, it will only be for ulterior motives; that is, because they have something to gain.

"Know thyself" is not the credo of a malignant narcissist.

In the end, malignant narcissists don't take responsibility for their actions, and, all in all, it is advisable to stay away from them. They will make others feel bad for being angry at them when they do them wrong. Those who remain close to the malignant narcissist will only end up feeling depleted—emotionally, mentally, spiritually, and probably financially. Whatever they do, it is never their fault. As a result of their emotional shallowness, they are essentially devoid of all empathy or compassion for others. Lacking empathy, they are very destructive and dangerous people to be around. Emotionally, they can be considered brick walls, able to see and hear others but failing to understand or relate to them. They will break the spirit of the people they deal with. When meeting and falling into the gravitational pull of malignant narcissists, people may have to learn, and incorporate, significant life lessons such as how to create boundaries, how to maintain their sense of self-respect, and how to be resilient.

Xavier, and others like him, are afraid that an inner journey will expose them as fakes and that others will realize that behind all the aggressive, self-confident posturing, there is really very little to show and that their growing arrogance is just a protective cover for their many insecurities. They are thus only prepared to see a grandiose image of themselves, not their true inner self. All they care about is this image, not who they really are. But by aggrandizing their own abilities and achievements, those suffering from malignant narcissism remain out of touch with who they truly are. What they really are all about has no real presence in their world. And as a reaction to their defective self, they tend to "project" their anxieties onto others. They will accuse others of what they fear in themselves. Again, these dramatic antics should also be seen as manic maneuvers to fill up their inner emptiness. They're looking for attention in whatever shape it may be, good or bad. The worst pain for these narcissists is to not be noticed. Consequently, if they are feeling ignored, they will say or do outrageous things to be seen.

Malignant narcissists are only prepared to see a grandiose image of themselves, not their true inner self. All they care about is this image, not who they really are.

In fact, the Xaviers of this world seem to be hampered by a lack of adjustment between their psychobiological needs and the care that had been provided to them. A lack of real attention from their caregivers at an early age has resulted in a great need for attention and has left them with a lack of an inner core. This emptiness inside—this feeling of never feeling good enough—needs to be filled constantly. It is no wonder that they are so unbalanced psychologically; that they possess such an unstable self-image, needing constant reinforcement; that the pursuit of self-realization has turned into self-absorption. In the process, other people have lost their value, becoming mere means to the fulfillment of these individuals' needs and desires. Other people are only viewed as extensions of themselves. And if those with malignant narcissistic tendencies manage to attain leadership positions—through various Machiavellian routes—the consequences can be devastating. They will destroy other people's lives and do it with such stealth as to make their victims feel that it is actually *they* who are letting the perpetrator down and not vice versa. And as suggested before, if they don't get what they want, their wrath can be terrible. In a way, the behavior of malignant narcissists is the antithesis of leadership because leadership is all about serving others. They are everything but merchants of hope. To call them merchants of doom would be a much more accurate description. Effectively, to quote the philosopher Arthur Schopenhauer, "Where there is a great deal of pride or vanity, there also will there be a great desire of vengeance."[4] All in all, the malignant narcissist is better avoided.

If those with malignant narcissistic tendencies manage to attain leadership positions—through various Machiavellian routes—the consequences can be devastating.

NOTES

1   Erich Fromm (1964). *The Heart of Man: Its Genius for Good and Evil.* New York: Lantern Books.
2   American Psychiatric Association (2022). *The Diagnostic and Statistical Manual of Mental Disorders,* 5th edition, *text revision (DSM-5-TR).* Washington, DC: APA.
3   Otto F. Kernberg (1993). *Severe Personality Disorders: Psychotherapeutic Strategies.* New Haven, CT: Yale University Press.
4   Arthur Schopenhauer (1915/1851). Psychological revelations. In *Religion: A Dialogue and Other Essays.* Trans. T. Bailey Saunders. London: G. Allen & Unwin.

EPIGRAPH SOURCES

Ovid (1929/2 AD). *The Art of Love [Ars Amatoria], and Other Poems.* With an English Translation by J.H. Mozley Sometime Scholar of King's College, Cambridge, Lecturer in Classics, University of London. London: William Heinemann Ltd.
Alexandre Dumas (1848/1844–1846). *The Count of Monte Cristo.* London: Simms and McIntyre, Chapter 40.

8

WRESTLING WITH A NARCISSIST

No one who, like me, conjures up the most evil of those half-tamed demons that inhabit the human breast, and seeks to wrestle with them, can expect to come through the struggle unscathed.

—Sigmund Freud

Not Chaos, not
The darkest pit of lowest Erebus,
Nor aught of blinder vacancy, scooped out
By help of dreams—can breed such fear and awe
As fall upon us often when we look
Into our Minds, into the Mind of Man.

—William Wordsworth

I have touched on the subject of changing narcissistic behavior patterns in previous chapters, but here I take a case study approach to look at it closely. The first thing to note is that changing narcissistic behavior patterns tends to be an uphill struggle. Any type of change is challenging when people don't see the need for it, and, as narcissism is an ego-centric disorder, narcissists are highly unlikely to see the negative side of their behavior. If they are to change, they need to be prepared to adjust their behavior patterns and be committed to getting help.

Of course, it is much easier to work with "light" than with malignant narcissists, whose mix of narcissism and psychopathy means that any intervention will most likely fail. Malignant narcissists never believe there is anything wrong

DOI: 10.4324/9781003569855-9

with them. This may be down to mental impairment or maybe the lack of the neural equipment needed to empathize with other people. Even if they can be coerced into undertaking some form of treatment, they will run rings around any poor professional hoping to help them.

> Any type of change is challenging when people don't see the need for it.

THE NARCISSISTIC CHALLENGE

Peter, a partner at a well-known strategic human resource consulting firm, was asked by Andrew, an old client, to coach the CEO of a company where Andrew was the chairman of the board. Andrew explained that he had met John, one of the key members of the company's executive team, at a social occasion. When he asked John how things were going, John replied that he planned to quit because working in the company had become far too stressful.

John had initially found the organization a stimulating environment, and working there was a great learning opportunity, particularly the chance to work with Denis, the CEO. But what once had been a very supportive relationship had turned sour. At first, the two of them had absorbing discussions about new directions for the company, but now Denis just issued orders. And John wasn't alone. The other members of the executive team had the same experience. They were all exposed to long harangues about what they had to do. There was very little give and take. Dealing with Denis was like walking on eggshells and the working environment had become toxic. Many of Denis's insights about the future of the industry were brilliant, but unfortunately there were also too many occasions when his judgment was questionable. John found that although Denis's behavior wasn't endangering the future of company, it was taking its toll on his own mental health and he was looking to leave.

> Even if a malignant narcissist can be coerced into undertaking some form of treatment, they will run rings around any poor professional hoping to help them.

Andrew was deeply troubled by this conversation and turned to Peter for advice. As chairman of the board, was there anything that he could or should do? He had always had a good relationship with Denis and viewed him as very capable. At the same time, John's comments didn't come as a total surprise. As a non-executive director on various boards, he had been privy to a number of situations where a CEO's behavior had become worrying. He had seen CEOs change when power had gone to their head. Some of them had started to live in an echo chamber, hearing only what they wanted to hear. If Denis was going into narcissistic overdrive, could something be done? And, if so, would Peter be willing to take Denis on as a coaching client? Andrew had already suggested to Denis that, as he had such a stressful job, it might be useful to exchange ideas with a coach, and to his great surprise, Denis was up for it. Perhaps he saw having a coach as a kind of status symbol—but whatever the reason for his compliance, Andrew had leapt on it and given Denis Peter's name.

Peter had spent quite some time dealing with narcissistic behavior among senior executives. While he knew that a healthy level of narcissism could provide the motivation, drive, and focus necessary for success, he also knew that narcissistic behavior had to be kept within bounds. He had learned the hard way that most narcissistic people were only interested in themselves. He was conscious of the fact that while a low level of narcissism might be instrumental in a person's success, having too much could lead to dysfunctionality. Self-centeredness and self-importance could turn into a highly toxic mix.

Nobody can appear kinder or more charming than narcissists when they are getting what they want.

As mentioned before, narcissists lack empathy and are largely unable to acknowledge other people's needs and emotions. Also, they have an unassailable sense of entitlement—rules are for others, not for them. They are exploitative, unfairly or cynically using other people to their advantage, and their deep-seated feelings of insecurity lead them to control, manipulate, and dominate others.

Nobody can appear kinder or more charming than narcissists when they are getting what they want, but this kindness and charm swiftly give way to intimidation when they don't get their own way. However, much of this behavior is just an act of bravura. Narcissists invest a great amount of energy into getting the upper hand as a way to hide their feelings of vulnerability. To reinforce their fragile sense of self, they are continually referring to themselves—their status, their possessions, and their lives.

Narcissists invest a great amount of energy into getting the upper hand as a way to hide their feelings of vulnerability.

From a developmental point of view, narcissistic traits often begin to emerge during the teenage years as the result of specific developmental processes, with parental understimulation, overstimulation, or chaotic chil-drearing seemingly playing an important role. Narcissism is in many ways a response to difficult early experiences.

TAKING THE HARD ROAD

Peter was well aware of all of this and had learned from experience how hard it was to change people who were unaware of the impact their behavior had on others. Efforts to "fix" their behavior usually turned out to be a waste of time and energy. The characteristics that typified their behavior were exactly those that made it so difficult to help them change. Feedback was for others but not for them—they seemed to be completely satisfied with themselves. Peter also knew, however, that a quick way to make a narcissist drop all pre-tense of friendliness and charm was to point out the errors of his or her ways.

Nevertheless, one of the critical roles of a company board is to monitor, coach, and, if necessary, fire a CEO, so if Andrew's comments held any truth, something needed to be done to modify Denis's behavior. As he seemed to have many good qualities, it would be worthwhile trying to help him to become more effective. Who knows—he might be receptive to modifying some of his behavior.

A quick way to make a narcissist drop all pretense of friendliness and charm is to point out the errors of his or her ways.

After having met Denis—a meeting that went quite well—Peter got a clear indication of Denis's self-centeredness, and it was obvious to him that Denis needed a considerable amount of behavioral recalibration. The predominant scripts in his inner theater needed substantial revision. The question was how to go about it. How could Peter make Denis realize that all was not well?

As far as the company was concerned, their conversations revealed that, even though there wasn't a burning platform, innovation was almost nonexist-ent and the company seemed to be on "automatic pilot," milking soon-expiring intellectual property. Peter, who knew the industry, thought the company's position was worrisome, given that the competition was ready to enter its mar-ket. On a more personal level, he also learned that Denis was in the middle of a contentious divorce, with arguments centered on money and visiting rights for the children. Peter also sensed that Denis was challenged by the process of aging. He seemed hypochondriacal, busily visiting various wellness establish-ments, finding it difficult to accept any sign of physical decline.

After a time, Peter felt he might be able to move their exchanges beyond polite chitchat and discuss some serious issues. If Denis would accept that he needed to deal with a number of issues, Peter might even get him to pay attention to his inner world—to acquire more self-knowledge and self-awareness. If he was to get out of his narcissistic bubble, Denis needed to figure out what compelled him to behave the way he did and how his behavior affected other people. He needed to understand his major drivers and acquire a more realistic sense of himself—not easy: narcissism typically involves a departure from self-understanding. One tool that would help would be 360-degree feedback plus interviews with his close collaborators. This would present Denis with clear data about his strengths and weaknesses and the effect his behavior had on others and the organization. If he understood and accepted that all was not well, it would help him to make more conscious decisions. The more control he had over his ego, the more successful he would be in all areas of his life.

> Narcissism typically involves a departure from self-understanding.

After some cajoling, Peter got Denis to go through a 360-degree feedback process and to give him permission to interview a number of his subordinates. Denis's narcissistic disposition probably lay behind his willingness to go through this exercise and to find out whether other people recognized what a great leader he was. In fact, Peter doubted whether self-improvement was at the top of his mind. But, whatever his reasons, it would give Peter a hook, as the exercise would result in a vast amount of factual data that would point out what Denis needed to do to improve his interactions with the people he worked with. Yet, given the toxic climate in the company, the interviews were not always straightforward and not very often. To help Peter to get to the truth, it was also important to listen to what was *not* being said. Eventually, however, through this process, Peter believed he had formed a good understanding of the positives and negatives of Denis's leadership style.

Peter was aware that he should not focus on the negatives when he presented Denis with the data. Despite his developmental challenges, it was important to point out Denis's strengths. They needed to figure out together what activities gave Denis energy and made him feel good about himself. If Denis could articulate a sense of purpose and focus on what was *really* important, he would understand better the underlying reasons for his behavior, and his need to be constantly in the limelight might become less dominant. He might realize that his behavior wasn't really providing him with the satisfaction he was seeking and that behind his narcissistic outbursts was a sense of inadequacy. Clearly, Peter needed to help Denis to transcend his envious and competitive feelings and rewrite the scripts in his inner theater around themes like compassion, empathy, and social responsibility. However, Peter was also aware that achieving this was not going to be a walk in the park—most people tend to maintain the status quo by holding on to false notions of the self.

Most people tend to maintain the status quo by holding on to false notions of the self.

Over a number of coaching sessions, Peter pointed out to Denis that any time he was tempted to go into narcissistic overdrive, he should ask himself why he was experiencing these feelings. What were the triggers? Then, instead of blowing his own trumpet, he should redirect the focus toward his personal progress and growth experiences. Self-interest should be channeled into self-improvement rather than excessive competitiveness. In particular, Peter knew that the development of empathy and compassion for others had to be part of this "cure." He told Denis that he needed to practice putting himself in other people's shoes. This cognitive reframing would help him to reduce the negative feelings he experienced when he felt irritated and prevent him from "acting out" in destructive ways.

Basically, Denis needed to learn other ways of managing his feelings about himself. Appreciating the good things he had would be a much more effective way to boost his sense of self-worth and a great antidote to his desire for more. Another pathway to temper Denis's feelings of grandiosity would be to nurture humility and learn not to feel superior to others. A greater concern for those less fortunate than himself would help to shift the focus away from himself. The act of giving and generosity could result in a sense of satisfaction that presently seemed to elude Denis. Changing his mindset in this way may reinforce different kinds of behavior.

Over time, Peter's approach had a positive effect on Denis. He gradually became less self-centered; the compulsion to blow his own trumpet became a less frequent occurrence. Although there were times when he was tempted to revert to his old self, he could now recognize what was happening to him and was able to hold himself back. Narcissistic tendencies would always play a part in Denis's personality makeup, but his behavior became less demoralizing for others. So how did Peter do it?

THE PROCESS TO ARRIVE AT THE "CURE"

Creating a working alliance

The first thing Peter did was to build a "working alliance" with Denis. In any relationship with a helping professional it is of utmost importance to create an emotional bond based on trust and mutual respect. The quality of this bond is a reliable predictor of the likelihood of a positive outcome. Peter created a judgment-free zone within which both parties were prepared to work together to arrive at constructive change. That said, Peter was well aware that building a relationship of trust with a narcissist is always an uphill struggle and that very little is needed to derail it and trigger defensive reactions.

In any relationship with a helping professional it is of utmost importance to create an emotional bond based on trust and mutual respect.

Tolerating the emotional seesaw

Narcissists are hypersensitive to criticism, so Peter knew that calling Denis out about his conflicted behavior patterns would not be helpful. Narcissistic individuals perceive negative feedback as a personal attack, an effort to belittle them. Denis could take any form of criticism, even constructive, as a narcissistic injury and react with anger. Even so, Peter recognized that he had to look beyond the drama, ignore aggressive behavior, and not take it personally. It was important to hold himself back when Denis made inappropriate comments.

So, Peter had to be aware of Denis's attempts to manipulate him and knew better than to expect an apology when he made hurtful remarks. Rather than having a knee-jerk reaction when Denis tried to throw him off-balance, Peter would say something like, "I understand that you are feeling hurt and angry, but let's stick to the facts." Consequently, he ignored attention grabs, stayed calm, and focused on the facts. If Denis had a dramatic outburst of anger, Peter saw this as part of an act, a form of manipulation and attention seeking. It was clear to Peter that narcissists can thrive on negative as well as positive emotions. In fact, the mood changes that his behavior could evoke in others provided Denis with some kind of validation.

Narcissists can thrive on negative as well as positive emotions.

Using the "grey rock" approach

Peter was familiar with the way narcissistic people try to bait the people they deal with. Clearly, given their "emotional seesaw" behavior, they like to get into fights. But taking the bait would only add fuel to the fire. Rather than give Denis a taste of his own medicine, it would be much better not to rise to the provocation and instead come across as a "grey rock"—a metaphor to describe persistent non-engagement with abuse—deflecting it by appearing uninterested. If he played this role effectively, a narcissist like Denis would lose interest in trying to manipulate him.

Of course, while using the grey rock approach, it was also important *not* to ignore the narcissist. Detachment should be a matter of degree. Peter limited the exchanges and gave only short replies in response to Denis's dramatizing antics, limiting the intensity of the discourse. It was much better not to engage with his distortions of reality and simply say calmly, "That's one way to look at it," and leave it at that.

Boundary management

Peter knew it was important to set boundaries to stop the drama getting out of hand. For example, he had made it quite clear to Denis that certain topics were off-limits, and he stood by these boundaries. He knew, of course, not to expect a narcissist to honor them, as narcissists think of themselves as the exception to every rule. However, if Denis did violate his boundaries, Peter didn't stay quiet but took care to aim his words at Denis's *actions* rather than his character. There were times when he was forced to tell Denis that certain kinds of behavior were unacceptable. If Denis's words or behavior were hurtful, he said, "Do you think this is the right way to deal with these matters? This is not what our discussion is supposed to be about."

Staying focused

Ego and self-knowledge are difficult to balance. The ultimate purpose of coaching Denis was to help him achieve greater self-understanding. Peter needed to make Denis realize that his ego had become an obstacle to his success. Ironically, his belief in his own greatness might be damaging Denis's ability to develop himself further. His inability to see things from several points of view put him firmly on the dysfunctional narcissism spectrum.

Peter explained to Denis that he was less effective when his decisions were based simply on his sense of superiority, his impulsivity, and his desire for praise. He told Denis clearly and repeatedly that he was trapped by his ego. Given his past experiences, Peter had learned not to be led astray by Denis's defensive maneuvers when he didn't like what he was hearing. He knew that Denis would try to derail him so he could avoid taking responsibility for ownership or responsibility for certain actions. Consequently, he was always on guard against Denis's attempts to deflect him and steer their conversations off course. In these situations, he would stand his ground and redirect their exchanges, preventing Denis from monopolizing the conversation or changing the subject. If the conversation became too one-sided, Peter would end it and move on. He had learned that he needed to remain specific and, when necessary, to repeat important points, always acting respectfully toward Denis and trying to arrive at solutions. And to facilitate the interchange, before each meeting, Peter would put together a plan of action, and afterwards he would note the decisions taken in written form. Given Denis's talent for distorting facts, it was vital to document what had been said. A written record to which both could refer would be an effective way to show Denis that his efforts to take control wouldn't work and that Peter wasn't going to be derailed.

> Ego and self-knowledge are difficult to balance.

Socratic questioning

Peter had learned that the most effective form of communication when dealing with people like Denis was to take a Socratic approach, asking open-ended questions that challenged assumptions, clarified meanings, and revealed underlying principles. He knew that any attempt to dwell on past errors would get them nowhere. Narcissists did not benefit from hearing about a long line of dysfunctional behavior dating back many years. Instead, it was much better to stay in the present and remain somewhat neutral. Instead of telling Denis that he had been completely wrong in the way he went about a specific decision, it was much better to say, "Your approach has quite a few merits, but I don't see the situation exactly the way you do." Also, instead of forcefully suggesting a better way to do something, he might comment, "I never thought it was possible to do things the way you have done it. Your approach sounds quite good, although I wonder whether it could have been done somewhat differently." Also, certain formulations can take the wind out of a narcissist's sails, like, "I hear what you're saying, and I'm sorry to hear that you feel that way," or "I am on your side. And yes, this is a difficult situation. But we can work on this together." Obviously, "shoulds" and "coulds" needed to be avoided.

> Narcissists do not benefit from hearing about a long line of dysfunctional behavior dating back many years. Instead, it is much better to stay in the present and remain somewhat neutral.

While navigating these Socratic maneuvers, Peter had learned the importance of choosing the right moment to make an important point. He needed to carefully assess whether Denis was in listening mode; otherwise, the intervention could misfire. In the same way, he would adjourn meetings with Denis if he thought the interchange was going nowhere and would take a break when things were getting too emotional.

The sandwich tactic

Peter recognized that he had to give Denis critical feedback in small doses. The best way to go about this was to feed him a compliment–criticism–compliment sandwich: expressing praise, followed by something that needed to be said, and ending with a compliment. The challenge was to reframe an issue in such a way that Denis would think he still had the upper hand. This approach would satisfy Denis's need to be admired while embedding negative feedback within compliments. Peter reinforced this by simultaneously praising Denis for what he was good at. He discovered that the best way to move forward was to explain to Denis how different ways of dealing with certain matters would make him look good. Moreover, Peter knew that his chance of being successful would be greater if he could convince Denis that the desired outcome was Denis's idea.

> Unresolved trauma makes narcissists blind to the ways in which their behavior affects other people.

Being empathic

Despite all the frustrations he experienced in his interactions with Denis, Peter kept on reminding himself that underneath Denis's façade of arrogance was someone with a low sense of self-esteem and deeply rooted insecurities. He knew that despite all of his apparent self-confidence, deep down, Denis's lack of true confidence required the constant approval of others. So, to the best of his ability—and it could be difficult at times—Peter always tried to be empathetic, recognizing that unresolved trauma makes narcissists blind to the ways in which their behavior affects other people. Still, he tried hard to make Denis understand that impressing people is very different from being impressive.

Peter knew that what narcissists want most is to be understood and loved. Therefore, it was important to be very attentive and to indicate that he was carefully listening to what Denis said. He used empathic expressions in response; for example, "If I had been in your situation, I can imagine that I would also feel sad and angry," or "It is remarkable how you managed to deal with that impossible situation." This didn't mean he had to agree or disagree with what Denis had done, but to reinforce their relationship and build trust it was important to make Denis understand that Peter was interested in what he had to say. He also hoped that this way of interacting with Denis would be a learning example and encourage Denis to experiment with empathic reactions himself.

> Impressing people is very different from being impressive.

The use of humor

Peter used humor in many of his interactions with Denis to show him the contrast or incongruity between how he presented certain issues and how they were in reality. This was a subtle, less threatening way of offering feedback. Humor can also be a great antidote to hubristic behavior. Getting Denis to laugh at himself might be very liberating. As he had found out the hard way, people who develop a sense of humor tend to be less egocentric and more realistic in their view of the world, be humbler in moments of success, and feel less defeated when faced with difficult challenges.

> People who develop a sense of humor tend to be less egocentric and more realistic in their view of the world, be humbler in moments of success, and feel less defeated when faced with difficult challenges.

BEYOND NARCISSISM

As time passed, Peter was pleased with the way his relationship with Denis developed. He helped him to recognize the errors of his ways, to convince him that his narcissistic behavior risked creating a self-made prison and that nothing makes a person more miserable than self-absorption. He helped Denis to see that, given the way he behaved, he had been engaged in an exercise of self-sabotage. He also helped Denis figure out that the real problem wasn't always others. The basic problem was on the inside. His challenge was to transform internally, from being self-centered to more other-centered.

Nothing makes a person more miserable than self-absorption.

Peter's familiarity with the psychodynamics of narcissism had enabled him to effect this change. He knew what behavioral patterns he could expect and how he should react to them. His understanding of basic narcissistic qualities, and what caused narcissistic personality disorders, had facilitated the exchanges with Denis and helped him to explain—in a constructive way—how to behave differently. He had made Denis realize that the more he made the world about himself, the more miserable he was likely to be.

The narcissistic mind has a fantastic ability to trick itself out of its own best interests.

Peter had started his interaction with Denis with a full realization of how difficult such an intervention would be and that dealing with narcissistic behavior would always be a work in progress. There could be no end to introspection. It would take time to change ingrained thought patterns and habits. The narcissistic mind has a fantastic ability to trick itself out of its own best interests. His work with Denis showed that once qualities of character like self-understanding, compassion, empathy, curiosity, realism, and a well-developed sense of humor are firmly in place, people are more likely to stay grounded and less prone to excessive behavior. When narcissistic people have the experience of feeling "good enough," they might acquire the sense of satiety that they were fundamentally seeking. They will learn that more is not necessarily better and that satisfaction ultimately comes from within. Or, to use the words of Ralph Waldo Emerson, "Nothing can bring you peace but yourself."[1]

When narcissistic people have the experience of feeling "good enough," they might acquire the sense of satiety that they were fundamentally seeking.

NOTE

1   Ralph Waldo Emerson (1876/1841). Self-reliance. In *Essays: First Series*. Boston: James R. Osgood and Co., p. 76.

EPIGRAPH SOURCES

Sigmund Freud (1905/1901). *Dora: An Analysis of a Case of Hysteria [Bruchstücke einer Hysterie-Analyse]*.
William Wordsworth (1888, published posthumously). *The Recluse*. London: Macmillan and Co., p. 52.

9

INFLUENCING NARCISSISTS THROUGH GROUP DYNAMICS

One must have chaos within to enable one to give birth to a dancing star.

—Friedrich Nietzsche

Many ideas grow better when transplanted into another mind than in the one where they sprang up.

—Oliver Wendell Holmes

Insanity is doing the same thing over and over again and expecting different results.

—Anon.

Another way of trying to modify the behavior of narcissists is to work with them within a group setting. A group intervention activity—if they are prepared to participate in one—can be a highly effective way of creating tipping points for change.

GROUP DYNAMICS

To illustrate this process, take Daniel, a senior executive working for a large social network. His organization invited him to participate in a top executive leadership development workshop at his organization. One of the major reasons for considering a team building exercise was Daniel's behavior. Although everybody recognized that Daniel had talent, most thought that he

DOI: 10.4324/9781003569855-10

was really a handful. He had a knack of irritating people, largely because he could not stop talking about himself and monopolized every conversation. Clearly, Daniel wasn't a listener. Whenever someone else spoke, he quickly became impatient and tried to change the topic to something closer to his own interests. Wherever he went, he seemed to think he was the most interesting person in the room. It was as if his ego was a drum and this drum needed to make a noise to let everyone know that it was there. Basically, he took up too much airtime at every meeting. His ego occupied so much space that there was very little room for anything else.

> Daniel's sense of entitlement was as big as his ego, and his ego was twice the size of his brain.

Daniel's modus operandi was to devalue other people's activities while blowing his own trumpet. It was clear to his colleagues that he viewed most people as being far below his standards. This toxic behavior was not improved by his tendency to take offense over every trifle. As a result, even though there were times when his contributions were genuinely valued, Daniel's extremely self-centered way of doing things had become more and more of an issue. People who had to deal with him regularly had coined the phrase that his sense of entitlement was as big as his ego, and his ego was twice the size of his brain. Could anything be done to make Daniel more of a team player? His colleagues hoped that the leadership development workshop would be a way to help him better integrate with the team and become less self-centered.

I have suggested before that having a narcissistic disposition may be a prerequisite for reaching the higher organizational echelons. Many narcissistically inclined people are quite charismatic, a quality that can not only help them to get ahead but can also benefit the organizations they lead. However, although their drive and ambitions can be effective in moving organizations forward, excessive narcissistic behavior can hamper effective organizational functioning. Competitiveness can be a good thing, but it needs to be tempered by cooperation. Extreme competitiveness is no prescription for teamwork. Daniel was overly competitive. His determination to win, whatever the cost, didn't benefit the organization.

> Competitiveness can be a good thing, but it needs to be tempered by cooperation.

Daniel exhibited several characteristics of a narcissistic disposition. He had a strong sense of entitlement; when he didn't receive the special treatment he believed he deserved, he became irritable. He was unempathetic; it was difficult for him to recognize or identify with the feelings and needs of other people. He was thin-skinned; any comment he didn't like would be taken personally. He was quick to feel hurt, to overreact, and to become defensive. He couldn't handle criticism and, as a result, giving him feedback about his behavior would be quite tricky.

Despite all of his bravura, Daniel seemed to possess a very delicate ego. Accordingly, although he gave the impression of being extremely satisfied with himself, the reality was very different. One of his colleagues, rather a psychologically astute individual, when talking about Daniel once quoted the German philosopher Friedrich Nietzsche, who said, "Talking much about oneself can also be a means to conceal oneself."[1] She speculated that a deep sense of insecurity could be hiding behind Daniel's egomaniacal and noisy behavior.

I went into some detail in the previous chapter about the challenges of working with people with a narcissistic psychological makeup. Individuals such as Daniel are not collaborative unless things are done on their terms. Their lack of insight makes it difficult to relate to them. To make matters even worse, they usually refuse to acknowledge that they have a problem. People who believe they are better than anyone else are not quick to ask for help from others. And they are slow to learn from mistakes because they are incapable of admitting that they make them.

> People who believe they are better than anyone else are not quick to ask for help from others.

There are many forms of intervention psychotherapists and coaches can use to help change narcissistic individuals, but all involve a lengthy uphill struggle. As helping professionals are the first to admit, personality traits don't change quickly, if at all.

However, one of the more promising intervention methods to help these people change is the group dynamics approach, which has offered encouraging results. Compared with one-on-one interventions, group dynamics expose people with issues to more pressure points, forces that can facilitate change. Group dynamics bring not only conscious but also unconscious processes into play, and, if change is desired, unconscious dynamics in particular need to be addressed.

Of course, unconscious dynamics are also at play in a one-to-one setting. However, they become especially powerful while dealing with the group-as-a-whole. In that respect, the group-as-a-whole can be compared with some kind of web that catches the collective conscious and unconscious fantasies that play out among the members of the group. It builds connections, trying to make sense of thoughts, moods, behavior, and actions that initially come across as mysterious.

> The group-as-a-whole can be compared with some kind of web that catches the collective conscious and unconscious fantasies that play out among the members of the group.

The ideas that are caught in this web will display many different qualities—some influencing each other positively, others negatively. In fact, it will contain partially metabolized material belonging to all of its members that can pertain to physical concerns, sexual/sensual matters, attachment concerns, self-esteem issues, and basic emotions such as sadness, happiness, fear, anger, surprise, and disgust.[2] Specific interpersonal dynamics relating to issues of power and authority will also be an inevitable part of these group activities, providing insights about the functioning of the group-as-a-whole and each participant's behavior. Subsequently, given their verbal and nonverbal contributions, the behavior of each individual is put under the group's microscope, and in that way the psychological processes taking place within the group-as-a-whole can become important forces for change. Unexpressed feelings and fears see the light of day. Many normally repressed thoughts and feelings rise to consciousness. The discussions that follow this process help participants to arrive at greater insights about their particular way of behaving and lead to suggestions for change.

Sharing and accepting the inner worlds of others help to create a virtuous circle of trust, self-disclosure, empathy, and acceptance. And here storytelling enters the picture. An important part of such a group intervention will be the invitation to each participant to tell their story. It will be an opportunity to all to better understand the challenges that each participant in the group is facing. And storytelling gives rise to interesting conscious and unconscious dynamics.

When storytelling occurs, it appears that the mirror neurons of the people who are listening go into overdrive, helping them identify with what's being told.[3] In fact, the storytellers are transferring ideas, thoughts, and emotions into the brains of the people who are listening. It seems that the brain of the storyteller and those of the listeners are becoming synchronized. Due to the emotional appeal of a story, emotional connections are being made, a process of synchronization through which meaning and purpose will be shared, creating a common ground that will help make sense of the storytell-ers' thoughts and feelings.

Sharing and accepting the inner worlds of others helps to create a virtuous circle of trust, self-disclosure, empathy, and acceptance.

These synchronizing brain activities enable the participants of the group to step into the storytellers' shoes, allowing them to enter other worlds and to create new ways of looking at things. And, helped by their imagination, listeners to these stories become participants in the story. It is no wonder that stories create genuine emotions that evoke passionate reactions, emotions experienced not only by the storytellers but also by the listeners.

Thus, the members of the group will feel emotionally connected to the protagonist of the story. While listening to these stories, they might step out of their own shoes, get to understand the other person's point of view, and increase their empathy for the "other." To simplify, it seems as if stories bring people's brains together. In fact, reflecting on other people's stories creates the space to think about their own story. And having a different way of look-ing at what they are up against will help them understand what contributes to their challenges more clearly. In other words, in a group setting storytelling can become a powerful vehicle to transfer life issues to other people, assisting them in the act of sensemaking and helping them change. It becomes a force-ful way for all the participants in the group to challenge conflicted narratives by seeing these issues in perspective and bringing some distance to salient experiences.

From the reactions that the storytellers evoke, given the reactions of the listeners, they will be able to take hard look at the stories that they are telling themselves. It will encourage them to reexamine how their personal history and stories have contributed to their present-day problems. And this reexami-nation will be the first step in reframing unhelpful habitual patterns, to arrive at an alternative story about the challenges they are facing. They may be able to develop new narratives that honor their past while enabling them to face the future in a much more constructive manner. Subsequently, taking a new outlook on life—encouraged by the participants who have been listening to these stories—the storytellers will feel more empowered to make the needed changes in their thought patterns and behavior. They will be able to "rewrite" their life story for the future. It may help them to move toward a healthier outlook on life.

> Stories bring people's brains together … . In a group setting storytelling can become a powerful vehicle to transfer life issues to other people, assisting them in the act of sensemaking and helping them change.

By offering support, reassurance, suggestions, and insights, the participants in the group, dealing with the emotions that come to the fore during these presentations, will have a therapeutic influence. Helped by the dynamics that take place in the group, defensiveness will be reduced, making people more open to change. Subsequently, due to the suggestions made by the members of the group, these interactions will contribute to a greater sense of self-respect and well-being. This transformative behavior will be facilitated through the process of imitation, also an important feature of these group dynamics. Participants will identify with one another, providing a significant force that can foster change.

Essentially, in the interchange between the group-as-a-whole and the individual, the inside will affect the outside, and the outside will affect the inside. There will be an interesting exchange between the inner theater of the individual and the "acting out" of the individuals' scripts within the group-as-a-whole. The drama made up by the group-as-a-whole affects its individual members, and individual dramas will affect the group-as-a-whole.

> In the interchange between the group-as-a-whole and the individual, the inside will affect the outside, and the outside will affect the inside.

These interactions between the individual and the group were very observable when Daniel was the center of attention in telling his story. Gradually, through a process of self-discovery, encouraged by the other participants, he obtained many insights about himself. For example, it dawned on him that the outcome of his compulsion to be the center of attention brought about precisely the opposite result. Instead of generating admiration, his behavior only brought resentment. Clearly, his "me, me, me" attitude left no room for "we, we, we." Daniel began to realize that a very egocentric outlook on life made for a very lonely existence. In fact, a mind clouded by ego, envy, greed, spite, and resentment could hardly make informed decisions.

With the aid of these group dynamics, Daniel learned that there were many other realities than his own. Pushed by the other participants, and mirroring what they had been doing, he realized that he needed to give these alternative realities a chance to come to the surface. They included things that he didn't like about himself but had to accept were very much part of his character. Daniel came to understand that he needed to accept his shadow side, to integrate these various parts of himself in a more constructive way. He had to face all of the negative things about himself that he had been suppressing and hiding beneath the mask that he was reluctant to admit that he was wearing.

Helped by the interactive processes that took place within the group-as-a-whole, Daniel also learned that if he put the needs of his staff ahead of his own, his part of the business would have a much better chance of prospering. Instead of always blowing his own trumpet, he would be much better off putting his energy into encouraging his people.

In Daniel's case, the group dynamics processes proved to be a great force for change. Taking a more conceptual point of view, six principal factors contributed to this transformation:

A group setting makes dysfunctional acting out more noticeable, more controllable, more discussable, and therefore less acceptable.

The team cohesion factor: A group setting makes dysfunctional acting out more noticeable, more controllable, more discussable, and therefore less acceptable. In many instances, peer pressure (Daniel being a good case in point) will push narcissistic people to adapt to the group's norms. In fact, "outliers" tend to change their attitudes or behavior to align with the opinions of others in the group. Subsequently, their peers take on the role of "enforcers." They will point out when a member of the group goes into narcissistic overdrive or when behavior becomes unacceptable. They will also encourage the narcissist to listen to and empathize with the others. These specific group dynamics enhance the traditional bi-personal dynamics found in other kinds of change processes.

The storytelling factor: By telling a story in a group setting, the participants are able to plant ideas, thoughts, and emotions into the brains of the other members of the group, making them share their grief, joy, and hardships. The stories told create a timeless link to other people's lives and experiences. Thus, through listening and telling stories, the participants learn about compassion, empathy, tolerance, and respect. And these emotional dynamics can be highly influential. They can change the way one thinks and even behave, narcissists included. In this case, the stories told, and the telling of his own story, helped Daniel to become more compassionate and empathic.

The team feedback factor: Helped by the storytelling process, narcissists seem to find it less threatening to receive feedback from a number of people rather than from a single person or the group leader. And, as could be seen in the case of Daniel, they also find group feedback much harder to ignore. Also, if the dynamics of the group are facilitated effectively, the narcissist's view of him- or herself will be revealed, mirrored, and challenged and thus can be modified.

The transitional space factor: Transitional space lies between internal and external reality. In this "twilight zone" between inner and outer worlds, between fantasy and reality, creative ideas have an opportunity to flourish. Transitional space can be looked at as an intermediate area where people are able to "play." It is very much up to the facilitator to create this "transitional space"—an environment in which narcissistic people like Daniel learn to develop trust, explore boundaries, and accept feedback, working toward greater self-understanding.[4] If the facilitation is done appropriately, the other participants in the group will be able to constructively confront problematic behavior while simultaneously offering a modicum of understanding. In this creative "playground," narcissistic individuals can become unstuck and use the space to modify their problematic behavior patterns.

> Transitional space lies between internal and external reality. In this "twilight zone" between inner and outer worlds, between fantasy and reality, creative ideas have an opportunity to flourish.

The group-as-a-whole factor: In Daniel's case, the group facilitator was very careful not to confront him too forcefully when he acted inappropriately during the group leadership development sessions centered around storytelling. When required, the facilitator would empathize with Daniel if he showed surprise or hurt after confrontations with and feedback given by his peers. At the same time, the facilitator empowered Daniel's peers to resist his way of dominating conversations, to be prepared to interrupt him when he went on for too long, to make him realize that he didn't always need to be the smartest person in the room. This at times confusing—at least to Daniel—interaction process forced him to take a more in-depth look at his behavior. He came to realize that by aggrandizing his own abilities and achievements, he was both out of touch with who he truly was and prone to cross the boundary of what other people considered acceptable behavior. Helped by the others in the group, he learned to make peace with himself. He recognized the value of experimenting with different types of behavior.

The road to insight: Aided by these group processes, over time Daniel learned to empathize with others. He realized that not everything was about him.

And as he practiced listening, he learned from others' experiences. He discovered that constructive criticism from others could be helpful, rather than considered a threat to his sense of self. Eventually, given the power of these group interactions, he recognized the inappropriateness of much of his behavior. He began to internalize some of the behavior patterns of the others, which, he discovered, would be much more effective ways of dealing with life's challenges.

Exposed to these group dynamics, Daniel's habitual defense mechanism started to crumble. Step by little step, he began to revise his ineffective beliefs and behavior patterns. The subtle sense he had always had that something was amiss in his life led to a gradual alteration of his conscious thoughts and his outlook on life. His newfound ability to get his ego out of the way had a substantial impact on the organization. Daniel learned that whenever his need for success and fame came to the fore, it was a warning sign that he needed to pause, reflect, and act differently. He had discovered that it gets pretty lonely with only your ego for company. Gradually, Daniel learned to become more team oriented and that his ego trips were journeys to nowhere. Later, he compared this process of checking his ego, abandoning it, letting it go to recovery from addiction.

It gets pretty lonely with only your ego for company.

So, Daniel's case became a success story. Nevertheless, dealing with narcissists is always going to be a challenge, in a group setting or otherwise. But if the suggested group dynamics intervention is successfully applied and it helps to modify people's narcissistic tendencies, everybody in the organization will be better off. Due to group dynamics, all participants may acquire the self-awareness and self-knowledge necessary to make their organization a better place to work. It is great way for an organization to get the best out of its people.

NOTES

1   Friedrich Nietzsche (1917). Apophthegms and interludes. In *Beyond Good and Evil*. Transl. H. Zimmern. New York: Modern Library, no. 169, p. 90.
2   Manfred F. R. Kets de Vries (2011). *The Hedgehog Effect*. San Francisco: Jossey-Bass.
3   Giacomo Rizzolatti and Laila Craighero (2004). The mirror-neuron system. *Annual Review of Neuroscience*, 27(1), 169–192; Manfred F. R. Kets de Vries (2024). *Storytelling for Leaders: Tales of Sorrow and Love*. London: Routledge.

4 Manfred F. R. Kets de Vries (2019). *Down the Rabbit Hole of Leadership: Leadership Pathology in Everyday Life*. London: Palgrave MacMillan.

EPIGRAPH SOURCES

Friedrich Nietzsche (1896/1892). *Thus Spake Zarathrustra. A Book for All and None.* Transl. Alexander Tille. London: Macmillan and Co.

Oliver Wendell Holmes Sr. (1892/1872). *The Poet at the Breakfast-Table.* Boston and New York: Houghton, Mifflin and Company.

10

LIVING IN THE AGE OF THE SELFIE

I tell you that the universe might go to the devil so long only as I could go on drinking tea.
—Fyodor Dostoevsky

The mystery of life is not a problem to be solved; it is a reality to be experienced.
—Jacobus Joannes Leeuw

To be what we are, and to become what we are capable of becoming, is the only end of life.
—Robert Louis Stevenson

THOU SHALT LOVE YOURSELF BEFORE THOU THINK ABOUT OTHERS

In contemporary society the consequences of the narcissism pandemic can be seen everywhere. Out of all the addictions in the world, the compulsive need for attention is slowly but surely becoming one of the most dangerous. Narcissistic behavior can be seen all around us. It has been blamed for everything from overspending and rampant consumerism to the rise of self-help books; the obsession with selfies by the YouTube, Instagram, and TikTok generation; the increase in cosmetic surgery; and the rise of populism. Clearly, *Homo sapiens* is an imperfect creature, having not only many egotistical defects and insecurities but also an irresistible desire for looking at their best. And, obviously, the excessive use of social media feeds these desires for an illusionary self.

DOI: 10.4324/9781003569855-11

Homo sapiens is an imperfect creature, having not only many egotistical defects and insecurities but also an irresistible desire for looking at their best.

If we believe the cultural pundits, we have become a society increasingly focused on excessive self-promotion and self-glorification. The major culprit that's enabling these processes appears to be the advances in technology. Technological progress has set into motion a set of seemingly disconnected variables that include the shortening of people's attention spans, the polarization of ideological orientations in society, the spread of election engineering, and the worship of celebrities. Furthermore, these variables have been influencing the way people are processing information. In our digital society, we have discovered alternative ways to get people's attention. The internet has expanded and accelerated the circulation of images and rumors, setting the stage for a culture of misinformation. Clearly, as people's incitement will improve a company's bottom line, the social media gatekeepers have been going out of their way to create the best "engagement factors," finding increasingly creative ways to keep their audiences hooked. Yet, with these efforts of seduction, whether something is a truth or a falsehood has become irrelevant.

All of these societal developments have been fueled by an intense focus on the self, increasing people's sense of entitlement, nurturing emotional immaturity, and, helped by confirmation biases, enabling people to live in bubbles of their own making. In the meantime, as a result of these regressive developments, critical thought has fallen by the wayside. Instead, societies have been created that are permeated by what can be best described as a "disorder of superficiality." The way the world is moving forward, it is trending toward even greater shallowness—at work, at school, at play, in parenting, and in love. Sadly, this narcissistic propensity toward superficiality is no longer looked at as exceptional. Keeping up appearances seems to be what the new world order is all about. The more exhibitionistic, vain, pretentious, seductive, manipulative, greedy, exploitative, or outrageous people can present themselves, the more attractive they become. Illustrative of these developments are attention-seeking celebrities, digital oversharing, and the boom in cosmetic surgery. Naturally, in this culture of self-exultation, there is little or no room for more altruistic, pro-social, community-oriented activities and, consequently, due to these sociocultural developments, many in society have lost their historical bearings.

Societies have been created that are permeated by what can be best described as a "disorder of superficiality."

Of course, most people are, at heart, egocentric. All of us exist at the center of our own little universes. Each of us is tempted to put ourselves ahead of others because we live under the illusion that we are significant. After all, we need to attend to our own needs, desires, wants, and aspirations, because, from an evolutionary perspective, survival has always been our greatest priority. Therefore, it should come as no surprise that no one else cares for us as much as we do. However, again taking an evolutionary perspective, it is important that this human desire to be self-centered be tempered with a community orientation.

In our present narcissistic age, however, the value of cooperative attitudes is being undermined. Self-centeredness has become overly important. Many people feel increasingly entitled to things—feeling that they are entitled to them, even though they are not prepared to make a *real* effort to attain them. They believe that they have the right to do or have what they want without having to work for it, under the presumption that they deserve whatever they are striving for just because of who they are. In the meantime, the value of discipline, self-regulation, loyalty, and community has diminished in importance.

Sadly, in the midst of this narcissistic pandemic, relationships have taken the hardest hit. As is now the case with material goods, many people seem to look at relationships as being interchangeable. Increasingly, people are taking leave of meaningful human connectedness and replacing it with branding, showmanship, and posturing. Driven by their personal desires, many are only looking for instant gratification—taking care of number one—without consideration of what this way of interacting means for others. The original checks against excessive narcissism, such as religious or civil values, have become alien. Religion, plagued by many scandals, seems to have abandoned its traditional role as the guardian of values. And civility has become merely a catchphrase.

Unfortunately, in embracing self-centeredness, people have forgotten that the cult of the self—living in a narcissistic bubble—has many downsides. As has been said before, it can get quite lonely with only your ego for company. Self-centeredness doesn't necessarily bring happiness. Selfish behavior will have a significant impact on personal relationships, causing harm and division between individuals. With it, the needs and desires of others are neglected, robbing people of the capacity to tune into and attend to others—contributing to social isolation.

People are taking leave of meaningful human connectedness and replacing it with branding, showmanship, and posturing.

Interestingly, predating these now apparent fallouts of the digital age, many of these concerns were addressed by the American historian and social critic Christopher Lasch in his seminal book *The Culture of Narcissism*.[1] Here he discussed a number of important social and existential themes, influenced by historical studies on anomie and alienation, starting with social scientist Ferdinand Tönnies' contribution, *Gemeinschaft and Gesellschaft*[2] and leading on to Émile Durkheim's influential book *Suicide*[3] and David Riesman's *The Lonely Crowd*.[4] In fact, Lasch echoed Riesman's critique of the "other-directed" personality in *The Lonely Crowd*; people who adjust their values to conform with their peer groups whom they resemble in age, social class, or otherwise. In other words, people who are not acknowledging traditional or inner-directed values but rather the shifting value systems of others. Therefore, it looks like our obsession with self-presentation predated the web by many years.

Given the societal themes that Lasch addressed, he could just as easily have been writing about the people of our present social media age who are strongly influenced by media platforms such as Facebook, Instagram, TikTok, X, YouTube, and LinkedIn—all of which foster a similar outlook on life. Nowadays, people who prefer to avoid the limelight have become rare. In that respect, the narcissistic orientation appears to be defining our present-day society as much as sexual inhibitions once characterized the Victorian age.

The narcissistic orientation appears to be defining our present-day society as much as sexual inhibitions once characterized the Victorian age.

Lasch's book delivered a damning commentary on the diminishing ability of modern society and culture to provide a sense of identity and security for its members. The catalysts for these changes, according to Lasch, were three structural transformative forces: the rise of postindustrial ways of manufacturing, the ubiquity of the mass media, and the transfer of personal, emotional labor from the family to the welfare state. These forces combined, he argued, were responsible for the rise of the narcissistic personality. In addition, he hypothesized that due to these specific socioeconomic changes, the late nineteenth and early twentieth centuries produced a culture in which the psychological pathology of narcissism had become normalized. According to him, narcissism had advanced stealthily into all aspects of society, and to clarify this point he noted society's fascination with fame and celebrity and the shallowness and transitory quality of interpersonal relations. These various changes—if Lasch is to be believed—had created a society unmoored from its historical pillars of status based on work, religion, achievement, or lineage. Consequently, due to these transformations, people had become caught up in a never-ending, never-fulfilling competition for the symbols of status. In other words, it had led to the release of people's inner Narcissus. As Lasch put it: "To live for the moment is the prevailing passion—to live for yourself, not for your predecessors or posterity. We are fast losing the sense of historical continuity, the sense of belonging to a succession of generations originating in the past and stretching into the future."[5]

An important part of Lasch's analysis was also leveled at the trend for self-help, which he saw as the search for competitive advantage through emotional manipulation. Or, to be more specific, he viewed the various trends seeking to promote "personal growth"—from self-help to spiritual movements—as driven by a narcissistic devotion to the self. In this context, he was also referring to the rise of "gurus," the increase in spiritual movements, and the growth of self-improvement programs such as EST (Erhard Seminars Training), Scientology, Primal Scream therapy, Transcendental Meditation, and Mindfulness training.

To explain these nonsecular developments and the weakening of the bonds of family and community, Lasch blamed both the political right's veneration of market forces and the political left's cultural progressivism. Pointing out that societal and character development tend to be quite interlinked, he suggested that these developments had affected character formation, which in turn had contributed to the rise of narcissism. Furthermore, Lasch suggested, once more referring to these linkages, that psychologists and social scientists had been interfering with traditional childrearing practices and that, due to the changes in practice that had occurred, the wisdom of the ages had been devalued, bringing all forms of authority (including the authority of experience) into disrepute. Fundamentally, authority was no longer what it used to be. And given all of these happenings—the result of people's frantic search for external validation—intimate relationships had become watered down. It is no wonder that Lasch considered the "me generation" to have become the new normal, a group characterized as infantile and selfish, one that demands rights but takes no responsibilities and that puts their own interests before any other consideration.

A few years before Lasch's seminal study about the rise of the narcissistic self—people too self-absorbed, searching for fame and celebrity—the American psychoanalyst and anthropologist Michael Maccoby published the book *The Gamesman*.[6] Here, Maccoby referred to a new type of CEO who was transforming the landscape of organizational life. According to him, these executives seemed to possess an unshakeable confidence in their own personal vision and suggested that these larger-than-life executives exhibited a personality type that closely resembled what Sigmund Freud described as narcissistic. Continuing his analysis of life in organizations, he pointed out that these narcissistic executives were the new heroes, celebrated from Silicon Valley to Wall Street. But he also warned that CEOs with these narcissistic personality traits might easily lead their organizations to ruin.

Returning to our own present-day society almost 50 years later, both Lasch and Maccoby made a number of observations that, if anything, ring even more true today. In their contributions, they performed the role of social critics by prompting us to look at our mirrored reflections, focusing on the question of whether we are more narcissistic than ever before. They insisted that not only had narcissism become more prevalent but so had its associated features like unrestrained self-indulgence, exaggerated self-importance, and, perhaps more important, a pervasive sense of entitlement.

The people that Lasch and Maccoby described appear to share a belief that they are extraordinary. They have an overinflated view of their own abilities. Unfortunately, however, what these people seem to have forgotten is that, in reality, most people aren't really extraordinary. Most people are human—all too human. Most people are full of flaws and imperfections. In other words, the problem with people who possess these narcissistic characteristics is that they have a very unrealistic outlook on life, a *Weltanschauung* that could come back to bite them.

In reality, most people aren't really extraordinary. Most people are human—all too human.

Of course, there is always the hope that as life progresses, the reality principle will set in, meaning that for many people, the belief in their own extraordinariness will sooner or later start to fade. However, this greater sense of reality could be accompanied by a greater sense of disillusionment—feelings that are hard to accept. It is unsurprising, therefore, that so many people will hold on to thinking they are extraordinary. They will continue in their merry narcissistic way. It is no wonder that it has become the new normal. And, given their behavior, it is not surprising that as a society we seem to have become somewhat desensitized both to the presence of narcissism and to the behaviors that accompany it; we may, in reality, have become too accepting of these behavior patterns.

So, considering these developments, what are some of the driving forces that have brought us to this point? What are the societal forces that foster this acceptance of living in a narcissistic society? Taking into consideration the observations of social critics such as Lasch and Maccoby, how can we reframe what's being said?

SOCIETAL FORCES

In the context of the narcissistic society, a critical development has been the move from *Gemeinschaft* to *Gesellschaft* (community to society)—a transformation that has had a considerable psychological impact.[7] In *Gemeinschaft*—community—social ties are defined on the basis of personalized social relationships and the roles, values, and beliefs associated with these interactions. In *Gesellschaft*—society—social ties tend to be more impersonal and rational, characterized by indirect interactions, formal roles, and generalized values and beliefs. Understandably, *Gemeinschaft* has been applied to peasant communities (families, tribes, or villages) within which human relationships are prized; the welfare of the group takes precedence over the individual; traditional bonds of family, kinship, and religion prevail; and personal relationships are defined by traditional social rules. In contrast, *Gesellschaft* can be viewed as being representative of a more urban, cosmopolitan society with a more individualistic outlook, where the connections are of a more impersonal, rational nature and social ties are more instrumental and superficial. In short, in these latter societies self-interest prevails, and efficiency and other economic and political considerations are given pride of place.

Accordingly, one way of explaining this increased focus on self-interest is to interpret it as a consequence of this transition from *Gemeinschaft* to *Gesellschaft*. These changes are seen as being responsible for the creation of a more individualistic, less community-oriented society, wherein the prevailing individualism will lead to a lessening of human connections, a development that could create increased feelings of loneliness—one of humankind's greatest fears. This increase in narcissistic behavior could thus be looked at as a form of protection against these troublesome feelings. In other words, narcissistic behavior can be considered some kind of defense mechanism to ensure people's mental health, an attempt to boost their sense of self-esteem. In fact, we could even look at the increasing levels of narcissism among people in our contemporary society as an ongoing adaptive response to dealing with the vicissitudes of life.

The rise of consumerism

Another contemporary societal development has been the rise in consumerism. Presently, many people now seem to be more focused on their materialistic needs. Conspicuous consumption has become omnipresent, as if human progress is equated with the conquest of resources. Unfortunately, with this perspective, people live under the illusion that these resources will be infinite—and so, too, consumption. Consequently, given this outlook on life, people seem to identify with what they choose to consume, a state of mind that can be described as some form of inward-looking narcissism. To be more specific, many people seem to display their self-worth through conspicuous consumption.

> Conspicuous consumption has become omnipresent, as if human progress is equated with the conquest of resources.

Unquestionably, emotional needs are difficult to take care of—or are almost impossible to satisfy—and material desires are much easier to deal with. It is so much easier to fill this inner void through materialistic behavior. Acquiring and consuming are much simpler means of self-gratification than investing in meaningful relationships and activities related to self-development. It is therefore no wonder why so many people pay the most attention to "visible goods" such as houses, cars, jewelry, clothes, accessories, and personal care products or anything else that displays status, power, and sophistication. Rather than a focus on more important matters, these consumptive activities have become a new religion. After all, it is so much easier to focus on these various status symbols designed to make people look well-off even if that may not be the case. And if we do not have the means, with the help of easy credit, we can all live with the narcissistic illusion that we are wealthy, successful, and special. Unfortunately, by attaining this sense of self-admiration through buying things they can't really afford, people are trying to ignore the reality of their situation.

The self-esteem movement

As touched upon earlier, another sociocultural development that has and is contributing to a narcissistic society are the changes taking place in childrearing practices—the foundation of sociocultural development. In recent years, many experts in child development have argued that in order to thrive, children need to be treated with unconditional positive regard. To explain this attitude, it could very well be that the parents' egos may be so fragile that they cannot bear the idea of dedicating their lives to the raising of children only to have them turn out ordinary. As extensions of themselves, they want their children to be as extraordinary as they believe their own selves to be.

Because of this mollycoddling attitude toward childrearing, there has been a prioritization of expressing feelings of self-worth, assuring children that they are special and amazing. Many parents will do anything to protect their offspring from any possible mishaps. Clearly, these helicopter parents, hovering over their children, are becoming increasingly prevalent in modern times.

These changes in childrearing practices are also reflected in the publication of books where the argument is put forward that parents don't really know more than their kids—a recommendation that makes them feel uncomfortable being placed in the role of authority figure. Parents would thus rather have their children *like* them than *respect* them, to be the child's friend rather than a guiding parent.

Parenting, however, is an incredibly powerful force for spreading cultural values. And an important part of the parenting process is the setting of boundaries between the dos and the don'ts, to help children understand what's permitted and what's not. After all, from their parents, children are supposed to learn what's right and what's wrong, how to treat others, to become familiar with political and economic beliefs, and to learn about prejudice and tolerance. Also, children need to understand that it will take effort to accomplish things in life.

Instead, taking the current perspective toward childrearing, the logical thought process is that it doesn't matter *what* you *do* but *who* you *are*. Yet, this assumption that children will be better off if they acquire a high sense of self-esteem may result in highly indulged children, at home and at school. After all, a short-sighted focus on building high self-esteem in children means unjustified praise by teachers and grade inflation at schools and universities. This approach will result in everyone being "excellent." Unfortunately, however great these children may think they are will not correlate with how great they *really* are. After all, when everyone gets an "A," nobody *really* gets an "A."

When everyone gets an "A," nobody *really* gets an "A."

This kind of parenting creates a situation resembling the story of the "Emperor's New Clothes." What we see is *not* what we get. The end result will be cognitive dissonance. The ascribed achievements are illusionary. In reality, life may not turn out as successful as had been promised. Instead, such an approach to childrearing is an invitation for the creation of a fake self. Given the divergence between fantasy and reality, people start to question their actual abilities. And deep down, despite a brave façade, all of this narcissistic maneuvering makes them feel incompetent. The outside world will see only the façade, not knowing that behind all of this self-love and self-confidence hides a deep sense of inferiority. The need to put up appearances, exacerbated by this kind of parenting and teaching, will contribute to a measurable rise in narcissism at the societal level. To make the situation even worse, all of this self-love will not lead to greater happiness. The people in question know that their appearance has no solid foundation, that they are "faking it"—a house of cards. It is no wonder that it is contributing to a higher degree of anxiety and depression.

The social media circus

A major contributing factor to this pandemic of narcissism has been the easy access to technology, especially the web. Presently, these digital platforms are woven into the fabric of social life. For this reason, narcissism has been able spread its wings and soar, riding on the social media outlets that have amplified and accelerated the process of image management. Clearly, social media appear to have infected the world with a sickening virus of self-absorption and vanity. Much of what's happening on these social networking websites is about satisfying people's egos and finding voyeuristic pleasures. They are quick outlets for attention-cravers, helping them to obtain an instant fix.

Narcissism has been able spread its wings and soar, riding on the social media outlets that have amplified and accelerated the process of image management.

Of course, one of the touted primary benefits of these sites has been the creation of social connection, which can promote constructive socialization, thereby preventing social isolation. In addition, they can provide ample opportunities to discover new information, learn about current events, and engage with issues, as well as enable people to have their voices heard. But the positives of these developments have not turned out as people would have wished them to be. What may have been considered a way of preventing social isolation may also contribute to exactly the opposite. More and more people feel increasingly lonely even though superficially—as suggested by their social media outlets—they seem to have many "friends."

By fostering social comparisons in the realms of attractiveness and being seen in the right place, the technology that drives these social media platforms seems to have been designed to foster people's narcissistic tendencies. And here it is important to remember that nobody is *always* at their best. Comparing oneself with others does not necessarily foster togetherness. Instead, it may create a feeling of being left out.

In addition, the addictiveness of these platforms should be highlighted. They encourage addictive behaviors. Features such as "like" buttons, notifications, and videos that start playing automatically make it hard to stay away from these sites. Adolescents, in particular, are impacted by these media platforms. But, at whatever age, these sites stimulate the brain regions associated with the desire for attention, feedback, and reactions from peers, reinforcing people's narcissistic tendencies and making for an endless reinforcing loop.

Given the state of technological progress, social networking sites have shaped how the younger generation looks at the world and, without doubt, artificial intelligence is here to stay. Specific skills people once possessed are now being taken over by the digital world: social media has affected the way people connect with each other, including the rather complicated interpersonal process called dating, which has been taken over by social platforms such as Tinder, Bumble, etc.; it is not necessary to learn to map read when apps such as Google Maps can do it for you and make route planning much easier; and why work on great report writing skills when they are easily replaced by ChatGPT? One could go on.

Of course, in previous eras, other media outlets provided an escape from reality by transporting consumers to the fictional universe of sitcoms, soap operas, and reality TV. Through the process of identification with the main characters in these plots, there was also some narcissistic enhancement. However, the digital environment we now live in makes for more blatant narcissism. In this age of digital narcissism, we are offered endless opportunities to brag about ourselves, to create inflated views of the self. Clearly, the digital world has become a great way of facilitating narcissistic, shameless self-promotion. Usually, the more exhibitionistic, vain, pretentious, seductive, manipulative, exploitative, or outrageous people can be on these media platforms, the better the ratings.

The digital world has become a great way of facilitating narcissistic, shameless self-promotion.

The unstoppable march of the selfies

Celebrity and non-celebrity alike, these many self-delusional activities appear to be unstoppable. Even for non-celebrities the recording of mundane events has become a way to prove their importance. In fact, the democratization of the media means that anyone with a smartphone can become a "celebrity." And it is selfies that help such people stay in this self-delusionary state. Whereas in the past nobody had even heard of a selfie, today every smartphone has not one but frequently two or more cameras, enabling its user to take (often idiotic) pictures anytime and anywhere. The manufacturers of these phones have realized how easy it is to turn vanity into a profit. Helped by this technology, exhibitionism and voyeurism have been reaching new heights. From a social psychological standpoint, by posting selfies to get attention, people can keep themselves in other people's minds. And through the clothes they wear, their expressions, their staging of the physical setting, the style of the photo, etc., they can convey a particular public image of themselves.

Of course, the people portrayed in these selfies always seem to be *so* confident, *so* self-assured. But the reality behind these images can be quite different. All too frequently, when perusing social media, we are faced with illusionary imagery. We encounter imaginary rich people (who may have lots of debt), imaginary beautiful people (who have undergone plastic surgery and cosmetic procedures and with every perceivable fault edited out), imaginary celebrities (via reality TV and YouTube), imaginary genius students (with grade inflation, an overprotective upbringing under helicopter parents, and party to an education focused on self-esteem), and imaginary friends (within the social networking explosion). It seems as if real life has turned into an illusion.

BEYOND THE BEYOND

What has become clear from this discussion is that narcissists and narcissistic behavior have always been with us. Yet, only in today's world, given the advances in technology, has it become more prevalent. And even though some of these narcissistic activities can be viewed as rather harmless, this behavior can also have very destructive repercussions. It may have dawned on us, given the societal shifts from a commitment to the collective to a focus on the individual or the self, that it has become much harder to meet people's basic need for meaningful connections. The movement from what is best for the community to what is best for "me" has not been without consequences. The development of hugely popular social networking sites, such as Facebook or Instagram, has further changed the way people are spending their free time and the way they communicate. As things stand, people spend an increasing amount of their time on these "social" websites. Ironically, this development hasn't necessarily improved human interaction. It can be quite lonely when actively social networking. In fact, two-dimensional exchanges seem to be a poor substitute for more three-dimensional ones.

The movement from what is best for the community to what is best for "me" has not been without consequences.

As noted, what has added to this acceleration of individualism has been the rise of consumerism and "me" culture. People are focusing more on themselves, *their* image, *their* wants, *their* needs, before the needs of others. And all of these developments have turned people inward, making them isolated and unhappy and, despite loads of material wealth, having little in the way of true quality of life. The replacement of intrinsic values by extrinsic activities has affected character development—and not necessarily for the better—which begs the question how this rise of narcissism is going to affect the way our society will turn out to be in the future. Perhaps the time has come to make some important changes—to alter these developments. Instead of merely celebrating the ego, we may need to find another script. Trying to keep up appearances—to focus on externalities—signals decay on the inside. It could very well be that we need to put these ego and celebrity cultures to sleep and make a strong effort to awaken authenticity and genuineness. But this will be a battle we must all fight together to win back our humanity, not only for ourselves but also for our children. We should always be aware of shallow living—both in ourselves and in others. After all, it's only by immersing ourselves deeply in real life that we will thrive.

It's only by immersing ourselves deeply in real life that we will thrive.

NOTES

1 Christopher Lasch (1979). *The Culture of Narcissism: American Life in an Age of Diminishing Expectations.* New York: Norton.
2 Ferdinand Tönnies (1887). *Gemeinschaft und Gesellschaft.* Leipzig: Fues.
3 Émile Durkheim (1951/1897). *Suicide: A Study in Sociology.* New York: The Free Press.
4 David Riesman (1950). *The Lonely Crowd: A Study of the Changing American Character.* London: Oxford University Press.
5 Christopher Lasch (1979). *The Culture of Narcissism: American Life in an Age of Diminishing Expectations.* New York: W.W. Norton & Company, p. 5.
6 Michael Maccoby (1976). *The Gamesman: The New Corporate Leaders.* New York: Simon & Shuster.
7 Ferdinand Tönnies (1887). *Gemeinschaft und Gesellschaft.* Leipzig: Fues.

EPIGRAPH SOURCES

Fyodor Dostoevsky (1914/1864). *Letters from the Underworld.* Transl. C. J. Hogarth. London: J. Dent & Sons.
Jacobus Johannes Leeuw (1928). *The Conquest of Illusion.* New York: Alfred Knopf.
Robert Louis Stevenson (1882). *Familiar Studies of Men and Books.* London: Chatto and Windus, p. 164.

CONCLUDING COMMENTS: BEYOND NARCISSISM

That by which the great rivers and seas receive the tribute of all the streams, is the fact of their being lowly; that is the cause of their superiority.

—Lao Tzu

Id facere laus est quod decet, non quod licet.*

—Seneca the Younger

Reflect that life, like every other blessing, derives its value from its use alone.

—Samuel Johnson

HOW WILL IT ALL END?

As mentioned in previous chapters, in our contemporary society narcissistic behavior has become part of the new world order. Yet even though such behavior may be disturbing, this kind of behavior isn't really anything new. All of us tend to consider ourselves to be the most important people in the world. But in current society, these behavioral manifestations may have reached a new level. And, although human nature has not fundamentally altered, it appears as if the world we live in has changed dramatically compared with the past. We could well be seeing a different reflection when we look in the mirror. Clearly, it has become obvious that the digital revolution

---

* He deserves praise who does not what he may, but what he ought.

DOI: 10.4324/9781003569855-12

as portrayed by social media has given us the means to fall even more in love with our own image. It is for all to see that many people have become quite talented in having their images reflected in such a digital mirror, to be shared via the internet with the world at large. Illusionary as it might be, it has become an effective way of feeling special, or of feeling connected. Unfortunately, as much as people like to stand out, all too frequently the imagery presented doesn't reflect reality. Truth be told, many of these images seem to be quite fake, and much of what is seen on social media is merely make-believe. By accepting this unreality, we are left with a culture of superficiality, a sociocultural development that is permeating work, education, and parenting—in fact, it is affecting every aspect of life. And despite all of these efforts at community building in this digital universe, it doesn't make for a society where intimate relationships will flourish.

All of us tend to consider ourselves to be the most important people in the world.

As has already been made very clear, narcissistic behavior exists on a spectrum. To a certain degree, all of us have narcissistic qualities. A moderate dose of narcissism is, as mentioned before, important for reasons of survival and has always been a significant part of our evolutionary code. In that respect, narcissistic behavior has always been with us. The omnipresence of narcissism is nothing new. Thus, why are sociocultural historians such as Lasch and Maccoby so concerned? It could very well be the case that there are not more narcissistic people around but that, with respect to their presence, we are just more informed, more aware, more educated. And if that's true, are we really so much different from previous generations when it comes to being obsessed with success, youth, looks, status, wealth, and other underpinnings of achievement?

Perhaps, though we are accusing the present generation of being selfish, the only thing they may be doing is imitating and learning from their parents. It could very well be that the present generation—often raised by helicopter parents—has been made to believe that they have the *right* to have everything: to be self-absorbed, to be self-centered, and to be self-entitled. They may have been told that they're one of a kind; that they are very special. With this kind of feedback, it is no wonder that they are believing the hype by taking selfies and by spending much of their time on social media to gather followers. In other words, they may not be acting better or worse than the generations who have come before them, just somewhat differently. As digital natives, they have found other ways to express themselves. An outlet to deal with their inner narcissism is simply more readily available than it would have been for their predecessors. After all, given human progress, they're existing in a different world, in a society where different rules apply. So, that said, is this new way to deal with their narcissistic disposition something to worry about? Doesn't every era have its peculiarities?

Of course, a more controversial way of trying to understand this rise of narcissistic manifestations in present-day society is to see it as a reaction to people's concern of having to deal with a world marked by terrorism, global warming, nuclear threats, hunger, war, dysfunctional leadership, and pandemics. As a response, people may feel compelled to create an image of imagined greatness, worried as they are that the world as they know it could be falling apart. Consequently, as a form of distraction, they are driven to focus on material matters, including conspicuous consumption. Living for the moment seems a better option. The operative expression becomes I/Me/Myself. Hence, keeping such a reaction in mind, it could very well be that the march of narcissism is nothing more than an ostrich-like response to people's hidden insecurities. The consequence of such a mindset, however, will be that these people labor under a carefully cultivated fog of unreality. They engage in deliberate obfuscation of the facts on the ground. And in this context, the compulsion to construct some kind of superficial identity becomes a reflection of their need to stave off the existential dread of a meaningless life.

People . . . feel compelled to create an image of imagined greatness, worried as they are that the world as they know it could be falling apart.

Taking this observation to heart—this concern about the future of our planet or the "world as we know it"—could very well mean that the warnings contained in the Narcissus myth have become more relevant than ever before. And thus, as suggested previously, dealing with this concern by means of digital reflection may not be the answer. To engage in make-believe will only get us so far. It will not make these concerns go away. By pursuing only highly superficial activities, there is the danger that one may get stuck in the same destructive imaging process that enslaved Narcissus. To take the route of Narcissus is not the way to move forward, to build a community of thought, or to build a consensus on how to create a better future. Behaving like an ostrich with its head in the sand is not the way to arrive at a life well lived. The world of artifice, built on Twitter, Instagram, TikTok, and Facebook and the tallying of "likes" and comments, is not going to provide the emotional satisfaction needed for creating a fulfilling and hopeful future.

A DANGER ZONE

With more and more people going into narcissistic overdrive, what becomes worrisome is that critical thinking has been falling by the wayside. Authenticity and realness are being replaced by branding, showmanship, and posturing. Too often, only the exterior is what seems to count; the interior be damned. While people are spending unquantifiable energy supporting and maintaining an utterly and completely fake self—in denial of their true self—they are really trying to avoid a deep, dark, cold void. They seem to go through incredible mental acrobatics to maintain and sustain a false image of themselves, but, as has been suggested before, living in a society that advocates these qualities will destroy people's capacity for human connectedness. Clearly, a culture of narcissism is not a place where true relationships can flourish. Instead, in such societies there will be a lack of compassion and empathy and an absence of tangible connectivity. Furthermore, it will be a life lived within a pseudo-reality.

But will it be possible to evade the reality principle? Will it be possible to prevent regressive-like behavior? Is it possible to create a world that transcends instant gratification, a world where people don't feel entitled? And is it possible to modify people's narcissistic behavior, to strive for more mature ways of going through life?

Maturity means being able to accept that we will not get all rewards immediately. It also suggests the ability to control emotions, respond appropriately to situations, and behave like an adult while dealing with others. It refers to the preparedness to delay gratification—a key aspect of growing up. Maturity also means having a sufficient amount of self-confidence to face reality, not to wish away insecurities by feeding a constant stream of lies to ourselves and to others. It implies realizing that reaching certain milestones in life doesn't come without effort. Feelings of entitlement should not be at the top of our minds.

Clearly, feeling entitled, rather than trying, failing, learning, and accomplishing things, is not the way forward. In actuality, going through life with an entitled outlook can become quite toxic. Feeling entitled to success, regardless of whether it has been earned, doesn't come without costs. When people expect everything to turn out their way (regardless of the effort they have made), and if their unrealistic expectations don't turn out to be what they feel they deserve, they're bound to be disappointed. And such disappointment can threaten the sense of self of these highly entitled people as they may be forced to accept that they aren't so special after all—a disappointment that can often lead to outbursts of anger and resentment. Clearly, such emotional reactions don't make for good relationships. Furthermore, attention-seeking behavior will isolate such people from those who are important in their lives, again exposing themselves to the risk of feeling frustrated, unhappy, and disappointed.

Life isn't a rose garden. People need to accept that health, aging, and the social world will not treat them as well as they would like them to. And confronting these limitations to living is especially threatening to entitled people because it might violate a worldview of self-superiority. However, in the context of entitlement, what people need to face is that a narcissistic orientation to life is inherently dysfunctional and will become self-defeating. Most likely, it will also have a negative effect on their mental health. Past a certain point, when reality sets in—when encountering the first disappointments—such a narcissistic, entitled orientation toward life may become unsustainable. Bringing narcissism and its derivative, entitlement, to a more macro level, it is there for all to see how the world economy has been damaged by risky, unrealistic overconfidence due to the narcissistic, entitled behavior of certain groups of individuals.

Life isn't a rose garden. People need to accept that health, aging, and the social world will not treat them as well as they would like them to.

Hopefully, when excessive narcissistic behavior becomes dysfunctional, it will be an educational experience. It may teach all of us important lessons from life. From these lessons, we will perhaps come to realize the value of meaningful connections, the importance of self-respect, the role played by resilience, and when to set boundaries. Of course, being able to acquire these qualities will require a tremendous amount of self-honesty and self-discipline. In the context of narcissism, it will always be very difficult to deal with inflated egos. In that respect, narcissistic people would do well to appreciate the value of humility. After all, without humility, there cannot be humanity. In truth, given the way life unfurls, the experiences we have are all lessons in humility.

NARCISSISM AND HUMILITY

As has been suggested before, narcissism and leadership can be considered close twins. In this book of essays it has been pointed out that many leaders have strong narcissistic characteristics. Thus, knowing its darker side, humility becomes of even greater importance in the context of leadership. To be in a leadership position can be dangerous when humility is missing. With humility, leaders can be truly transforming; or, to quote the Indian poet/philosopher Rabindranath Tagore, "We come nearest to the great when we are great in humility."[1] A lack of it could lead us to the gates of Hell.

To be in a leadership position can be dangerous when humility is missing.

When leaders admire themselves too much in a mirror, when they show signs of pride, self-inflation, and conceit, these behavior patterns can be seen as external signs of an inner emptiness. Actually, a show of pride appears to be one of the most common covers of great insecurity. Prideful people will hide their insecurities behind a false persona of bravado, boasting of their inconsequential deeds, pyrrhic victories, and adamant refusals to tackle difficult tasks. In contrast, living with humility, and serving with humility, is one of the most important qualities for being an effective leader.

Clearly, humility can be construed as the absence of narcissism, self-enhancement, or defensiveness. We can look at true humility as a form of intelligent self-respect. With humility, people are less likely to think too highly of themselves. They tend to be modest as they remind themselves how much they have fallen short of what they could be. Or, to quote the Scottish novelist James Matthew Barrie, "Life is a long lesson in humility."[2]

Humility empties us of ourselves so that we can be filled with all of the things that we would otherwise never realize we had missed.

Self-understanding also plays a role in the context of humility. Indeed, the first product of self-understanding is humility. Humility empties us of ourselves so that we can be filled with all of the things that we would otherwise never realize we had missed. In that respect, we can counterfeit love, we can counterfeit faith, we can counterfeit hope, but, as we may discover, it is very difficult to counterfeit humility. However, without humility, as we have seen in this discussion of narcissism, there will be no humanity. By embracing humility, we can be liberated from the egotism that drives both perfectionism and self-sabotage, opening us to a deeper experience of self-worth. And even though it is important to have a solid amount of self-confidence, without humility this can quickly turn into arrogance. So perhaps a way to overcome overly narcissistic behavior is to become "in touch" with our humanity by really knowing ourselves. Here, self-awareness and self-knowledge—knowing why we do what we do and who we are—will be critical. In fact, there is very little need to show off when people know what they're all about; that is, when they don't have to present a false self.

> There is very little need to show off when people know what they're all about; that is, when they don't have to present a false self.

In a leadership context, one of the greatest feats potential leaders can accomplish is realizing that they're not so great, that they are merely human with all the frailties and imperfections that go with it. True humility derives from an appreciation that our time on Earth is limited but that we can contribute to activities beyond the self. Humility means recognizing that we are not on Earth to demonstrate how important we are. What's much more constructive is seeing how much of a difference we can make in the lives of others, or showing our humanity.

Being human means that we love, struggle, hope, and sometimes feel lost. We ask big questions like, "Why are we here?" and "What's our purpose?"—questions that will fill us with a sense of humility. But being human also has to do with personal development, growth, and fulfilling our true potential. Also, to be human implies having the ability to exercise compassion and empathy. And it is this combination of humility and humanity that often has helped *Homo sapiens* to change the world for the better.

A VIRTUOUS CIRCLE

Our discussion of narcissism began by putting the prototypical Narcissus of ancient myths on the analyst's couch and demonstrating what could go wrong. It was also pointed out that it could become the highway to perdition. However, it was also suggested that it didn't have to be this way. People *could* enter a very different highway. Reference has been made to people who have developed a healthy level of self-esteem, possessed empathy and compassion, and had humility. Here, we discussed people who tried to acquire greater self-awareness and self-knowledge. They are the people who realize that they have three different people living inside them each day of their life—who they were, who they are, and who they would like to become. An important aspect of feeling wholesome is the ability to recognize these different aspects of the self, to know who we are today. In fact, who we *think* we are and who we *actually* are may be very different and depend on how honest we allow us to be with ourselves. This is why our choices and actions speak louder than any of our thoughts and words ever will.

> Who we *think* we are and who we *actually* are may be very different and depend on how honest we allow us to be with ourselves.

Having taken this journey into the narcissistic world, I will end with the words of the German-American psychoanalyst and philosopher Erich Fromm, who once said, "The opposite pole to narcissism is objectivity; it is the faculty to see other people and things *as they are*, objectively, and to be able to separate this *objective* picture from a picture which is formed by one's desires and fears."[3] After taking this journey into the narcissistic realm, we can only hope that the lessons contained in the myth of Narcissus will convince many of us to take this route. Of course, the choice is ours. But what we should remember is that though we can always try to dress up our narcissistic disposition, we don't need to behave like a wolf in sheep's clothing.

NOTES

1   Sir Rabindranath Tagore (1916). *Stray Birds*. New York: The Macmillan Company, no. 57.
2   J. M. Barrie (1891). *The Little Minister*. New York: Lovell, Coryell & Company, Chapter 3.
3   Erich Fromm (1956). *The Art of Loving*. New York: Harper & Row.

EPIGRAPH SOURCES

Lao Tzu (1913/6th Century BC). *The Simple Way of Laotze (The "Old Boy")*. *A New Translation of the Tao-Teh-King*. Transl. Walter Gorn-Old. London: William Rider & Son.
Seneca the Younger (attributed; c. 4 BC–65 AD). *Octavia*, line 454. Author's translation.
Samuel Johnson (1796/1726–1749). *Irene. A Tragedy*. London: George Cawthorn, Act III, Scene 8, line 28.

Index

For Product Safety Concerns and Information please contact our EU
representative GPSR@taylorandfrancis.com
Taylor & Francis Verlag GmbH, Kaufingerstraße 24, 80331 München, Germany

www.ingramcontent.com/pod-product-compliance
Lightning Source LLC
Chambersburg PA
CBHW052013270326
41929CB00015B/2895